A Journey into S.E.N.D Motherhood

Finding the end of the rainbow

SEND Reform England

Print ISBN: 978-1-915626-11-0

1st Edition

Some names and identifying details have been changed to protect the privacy of individuals

Published by El Jedras Publishing House

Formatted by Nicole Bateman from A Box Full of Joy

Book Cover Design by Siobhan Little

Contents

** Disclaimer **

The Journey into SEND Motherhood: Finding the End of the Rainbow
contains raw and unfiltered stories from mothers who have navigated the world
of special educational and additional needs. These stories touch upon sensitive
subjects, including the loss of loved ones, miscarriage during pregnancy,
rainbow babies (a term for children born after a pregnancy or infant loss), and
the challenges of raising children with unique needs.

Please be aware that while these stories are offered with the intent of sharing
experiences and providing support, they may evoke strong emotions or trigger
personal memories for some readers. We encourage readers to approach this
book with sensitivity and self-care.

Our aim is to create a supportive and understanding community for SEND
mothers and supporters. Your journey, experiences, and emotions are valued,
and we hope this book serves as a source of inspiration, connection, and
strength.

If you find that any content in this book becomes too overwhelming or triggers
any distressing emotions, we recommend taking a moment to pause and reflect,
or, if necessary, seeking support from a trusted friend, family member, or
professional.

Please remember that you are not alone, and the SEND community stands with
you.

Introduction

When a woman finds herself as the mother of a SEND child, a unique journey unfolds; a transformational experience. Within the pages of this book, 17 mothers have united to share the raw, unfiltered, intimate stories that encompass the battles they have faced and the victories they have won. The stories that follow are the lifeblood of these mothers, each of whom has faced adversity with remarkable resilience and unwavering love. Their stories provide insight into the unique world of SEND, where they have tirelessly championed the cause, working hard to create a society in which every child, regardless of their unique needs, can not only survive but thrive.

At the heart of this book lies the national campaign group, SEND Reform England. This organisation, comprised largely of the women sharing their stories here, is challenging the currently underfunded SEND education system in England. The group was born of friendship, brought about by 11 mothers from across England connecting through shared experience over social media. Together, they realised that they were not alone in their fight for better services. The struggles they faced were not isolated incidents; they were part of a national crisis, and it was time for change.

Since its inception, SEND Reform England has grown beyond expectations, giving rise to a strong, passionate community. The group has organised 14 protests across England, made news headlines, delivered a petition with 80,000 signatures to Parliament, met with MPs and participated in the All-Party

Parliamentary Group for Autism. Their commitment to change is boundless, fuelled not only by the love that they have for their children but now also for each other.

Preface

(A word from the Authors)

In a few short months, SEND Reform England has been on an incredible journey and we aim to continue our work creating a community of voices that speak up for change in the SEND community. We have already done so much in such a short space of time and now, here we are with this book! All proceeds of which will contribute to the important work of SEND Reform England, helping us to achieve our goal of seeing every child and young person in an educational setting where they can truly thrive. We are honoured to also have parents outside of the organisation join us to share their stories and further our collective cause.

In our collaborative effort, we invite you to explore our personal stories. They will take you on a journey that is not just about us being mothers, but also about being women who have discovered new layers of strength, love, and advocacy within ourselves.

To our fellow SEND mums and supporters, we are delighted to welcome you to this book. It is a place where we can talk openly, without judgment; a safe place. Most people understand the challenges of motherhood, but when you add children with additional needs into the mix, it can become a daunting and lonely journey. We don't want you to feel alone. We want you to know that you are part of this incredible SEND community, a community that "gets it." This is exactly how our journey began. If you are searching for connection, inspiration, and understanding in the authentic voices of SEND mothers, then let our book be your guide. It will lead you to the end of the rainbow, where the colours of resilience, strength and love shine the brightest.

Chapter 1

SEND Help and Wine

Lisa Lloyd

'You're just an anxious parent!' Well, yes. No shit Sherlock. I'm anxious because my child is autistic and no one is listening to me!

The thing is, when you are constantly being told your child is fine and it's your parenting, you start to believe it. That is until you see the meltdowns and then you become certain again - no, this isn't the norm.

So I made a decision to not let it go and to become one of those annoying parents that the schools and doctors hate. I mean, let's be honest, doctor's receptionists hate everyone anyway.

Fin was referred by the Health Visitor at age 2 and was finally diagnosed with autism at age 6. I sobbed. I wasn't crying for the fact he had autism, it was the relief of finally being heard. The relief of knowing I wasn't going crazy. 4 years of being turned away, or having people make you feel like you are going crazy - to all be over within a couple of hour's appointment.

The Doctors knew pretty much straight away at the assessment. For one thing, he wouldn't look at them or say hello. Then when they tried to get him to play, he ignored them completely and only wanted to talk about his special interest. I think at that time it was zombies, and surprisingly there aren't many zombie toys in a doctor's surgery! I was secretly pleased he wasn't engaging as I needed them to see this. I was sure he was going to walk in and shake their hand - just to make me look like a fucking idiot.

Anyway, once we received the diagnosis, I held my breath waiting for the golden documents. Surely we must be given support now. Would we have our own personal support person? What meetings would be arranged? Maybe a list of schools he can now attend suited to his needs? The Doctor then handed it to me. The leaflet. I looked at it to see what vital information this would be. And guess what it was? a copy and paste of a Google search of autism. And that was it. We skipped off into the distance with no support and ready to start the next battle of getting an EHCP.

During this time however, we had Poppy and what an entrance she made. She screamed constantly, which the doctors said was silent reflux and colic, she wouldn't feed so was dropping weight fast and had a giant birthmark on her arm which meant due to its size, she had to have a brain scan. I have to say that this was probably one of the darkest times in my life. Fin had just been diagnosed and Poppy was a newborn who screamed constantly. The guilt I had for Fin was overwhelming. I couldn't cater to his needs as I was too busy trying to pacify Poppy in order not to keep causing Fin to have meltdowns. I was drowning.

The depression took over. I wasn't enjoying parenthood. It's a really hard thing to admit as you feel so guilty for saying it. People in the world are unable to have babies and here I am, wishing mine away. When I was starting to have thoughts that I didn't want to be here anymore, we knew it was time to seek help. I was put on antidepressants and suddenly I could cope again. It's something I have realised I don't need to be ashamed of. If you have a headache, you take medicine for it. I had a hormonal imbalance - medication is sometimes the only answer.

But thankfully, after several hospital trips and weaning her early, Poppy turned into a happy baby. Very social and responded well. The complete opposite to Fin. Fin was known as the Victor Meldrew baby - he came into the world pissed off with everything and that has continued since. I mean, who can blame him? But because of this attitude I assumed all autistic babies must be serious and therefore Poppy obviously isn't. How wrong I was.

Around the age of two, Poppy had no speech, she seemed in a daydream constantly and never responded to her name. There were definite sensory issues with food in particular and then came the flapping and tiptoe walking and I thought, here we go again!

Once again, the intrusive thoughts started. It must be my parenting now that I have two autistic children! What are the odds? Obviously now I know better and that it can be genetic but at the time I was clueless. And clueless is something I have been many times. Poor Fin was basically my guinea pig. The problem is there is no rule book, the only way to learn is by going through it.

One of the times that haunts me is when taking Fin to a family party. This was before he was diagnosed and I didn't know what I was dealing with. The music was loud, the disco lights were blaring and people everywhere. Sensory hell. The way Fin coped was to sit in the corner rocking his toy car back and forth. I looked around at the other children dancing and interacting with each other and wondered why is that not him? I was upset, angry even. So I took the car from him. I thought I could force him to behave like the others. Of course, what I had actually done was removed his safety. This led to a huge meltdown. I then sobbed. I knew we could never experience parties like others, we would always be limited with what we could do and where we could go. Completely selfish thinking but I was sad for myself at that moment of time.

I know now that this is ok. I was allowed to fuck up. We make mistakes and learn from them. And the biggest lesson learnt since having these amazing kids is to not give a damn what others think. It takes time and work to get there though.

Did I get stares when Poppy walked around the supermarket barefoot with her shoes on her hands making dinosaur noises? Yes, of course! But I came to realise that the stares were far easier to take than dealing with a meltdown from stopping her. The staring won't follow me home but unfortunately her meltdown will. So it all comes down to picking your battles. Will it hurt them? Will it hurt someone else? No? then it's probably fine. Some call this lazy parenting - I call it smart parenting. The thing is, until you have children with additional needs you will never really get it. I admit, before having Fin I was the smuggest parent you could get. My child was only ever going to eat healthy meals, limited screen time and read the whole works of Dickens before the age of two. Isn't it weird how the perfect parents who know everything are always the ones without children?

I think that's one of the hardest things of raising SEN children, most of the things that we do, go against the social norm or the perfect parenting books. Not because we are shit parents but because we have had to adapt to our child's needs. It's easy for someone to look at our child eating nuggets for every meal and tell us that we are doing it wrong. Force feed them! Let them go hungry if they won't eat healthy! But the raw truth is, when you have watched your child dropping weight and was almost tube fed, you don't care what they eat as long as they eat! It's not fussy eating, it's severe sensory issues. And it's just one thing on a huge list of our worries. And worrying is something I have become a pro at. I worry about my children having friends. I worry what their life will look like as they become an adult. I worry if they will ever sleep again (said whilst sobbing silently) I worry if they will be bullied. I worry if they are happy. Even understanding when they are happy was a huge learning curve for me.

I remember us taking Fin to Cbeebies land. We were so excited because he was crazy about Cbeebies and watched it constantly. But his reaction was not what we were expecting. We took him on the Iggle Piggle boat and as we rode past all the children squealing with delight, we looked at Fin's face which resembled someone who had just discovered their dog had shat in their shoe. We thought he must be having a horrible time, until we got home and he didn't stop talking about it. It hit us like a ton of bricks - he loved it but just can't express happiness the way we do. This can be tricky to explain to people. Especially with the dreaded birthdays. He will possibly throw your gift - please don't take it personally. He probably really loves it. But it doesn't matter how many times you explain it to family and friends, you can still see they look disappointed. I think this led to my anxiety with us meeting family. My children will never run into their grandparents arms telling them they love them. For some people this is too hard to accept. And sadly you may lose some family and friends along the way. I say sadly as in for them because they will never know the joy these amazing kids can bring. They will never work hard enough to gain their trust and have a bond for life from it.

So over time, it can become a lonely journey. You start looking around at your village getting smaller. Days out with neurotypical families seem impossible - you can feel like a burden on people. I can't have a conversation with you, whilst making sure my kids are not killing each other or themselves. I can't travel too far as I know the kids will be beside themselves by the time we even get to you. We can't do sitting down - so we can't do eating out, theatre trips or picnics. So I end up saying no a lot and eventually the invites stop. This is a tough pill to swallow. It's lonely as a parent with very little adult conversation, even lonelier as a SEN parent with no babysitters, no holiday clubs and no break. And a mum with no break, can become a mum on the edge. Depression, anxiety, not to mention losing herself. Even relationships can struggle. I am lucky to have Terry, the most amazing partner you could ask for. But even we don't get a date night. A date night to us is getting a cheeky takeaway and having an early night. Not for sex but to literally catch up on some sleep. I even found myself watching Peppa Pig after they had gone to sleep one night for Christ sake, I didn't realise until I was half an hour into it. I mean, it was a good episode but I'm pretty sure it's just Stockholm Syndrome and these kids are running the joint. I'm just a slave.

I don't want you to think that I don't like my kids as I love them more than I've loved anything before. But it's hard and as parents we are allowed to admit that. When you start thinking of having children, you don't expect to be raising disabled children. You expect that by certain ages you will begin to get your life back. You never imagine wiping bums at the age of 11 still or cutting their food up into teen years.

But even though the tough days are awful, I honestly wouldn't change them for a thing. I love their quirky ways, I love that they tell people exactly what they think - if only everyone was more like this! I won't lie, at times I have wanted the ground to swallow me. I remember Fin telling our friend that her house was dirty and another time he announced in the shops that I farted. Not to mention Poppy grabbing a lady's back fat in the changing rooms and shouting 'boobies' at the top of her voice. I usually pretend they are not with me but it's really difficult when they start calling me mum. But even so, they have taught me so much about myself. I have now been referred for autism. I see so much of myself in them, I was the one who never fit anywhere at school. Maybe life would have been different for me if I understood who I was better. But as always, the waiting list is long so I will possibly be 80 by the time they actually get around to seeing me.

And as they have got older and I understand their ways more, I've realised the hardship was never really them. It's the rest of the world. I had been trying to make these incredible little neurodiverse minds fit into a world not built for them, a neurotypical world. All I had needed to do all along was accept them and change the world around them. And once I gained this knowledge and confidence, I found my people through social media. I started to talk about our journey and found thousands in the same position. Thousands of parents lost and unsupported during and after the diagnosis. Thousands being ignored. Thousands struggling but too afraid to admit it because they felt they had failed somehow. And then some who wanted to change the world like me. Some who decided we were no longer going to accept less than equality for our children.

I found my people.

My village.

And this SEND village is incredible.

Lisa Lloyd

About the Author

Lisa is a mum of 2 autistic children who has campaigned tirelessly for SEND Reform. Lisa's love language is humour, and she brightens the days of so many through her social media account: ASD with a G & T.

Lisa's greatest fear was that her autistic children would struggle to find friends, which has made Lisa become the loyal friend everyone wishes for. She is relentless when it comes to acceptance and change for good although her love and commitment to a good cup of tea is just as powerful. She is a content creator, and one of the founders of SEND Reform. Having done a skydive for Mencap and swam with sharks, she can confirm that motherhood is the scariest thing she has ever done!

Chapter 2

The Snowy Haired Boy and Me

Layla Twinn

A fter what felt like the longest pregnancy ever which was full of sickness, hospital stays and a huge dab of denial that I was having a baby, my induction day finally arrived.

It was the 30th of October the day this baby would be born. After being induced and a very quick labour of two hours and 15 minutes compared to my first, which was a toe curling 16 hours, baby Milo Hulk smashed his way into the world. As the midwife laid this tiny white-haired baby on my chest, I looked up at her and said 'why is his hair so white? Is he Albino?', She laughed at me and replied, 'no, he is perfect'. I muttered back 'I didn't say he wasn't perfect'. I then asked 'is he in shock then? Why is his hair so white?' Again, I was told he was fine. After a short while a Paediatrician came to see him due to breathing issues, again I asked the question 'is he Albino?'. Again, I was laughed at. They then whisked my tiny baby down to the NICU with me sat there in shock. I did not see him again for nearly 24 hours due to me being very poorly.

Milo's Dad was a trouper going back and forth between me and Milo in the NICU, I remember he said, 'his hair is looking more blonde'. I demanded he take me to see him and against the advice of the Midwife team he took me to meet my baby. As he wheeled me into the room Milo was laying on his tummy in an incubator with a feeding tube in his nose, cannula in his tiny hand, and a monitor on his foot. I placed my hand through those little holes and stroked his back, his hair still white. In fact, he was super hairy, he had a little line of white hair going down his back and his eyebrows joined his hairline. He looked like a little wolf. I asked the nurse in the room if she felt his hair was a funny colour and asked the Paediatrician but again, I was shut down.

Sat back on the maternity ward I began to Google. I found that Albino is an outdated term, and the condition is called Albinism. I went into a bit of a rabbit hole finding horrific stories about people with Albinism in Africa, being not very mobile and without my baby, Google became my friend. With everyone telling me Milo did not have Albinism, I messaged two of my close friends who I knew I could trust to tell me the truth. One a GP and the other an Area SENCo, so professionally as well as being my friends I knew they'd give me a truthful answer. That answer was YES! They thought the same as me. Which made me feel like I was not creating something in my head. It was real, there was something there.

By three days old we got a new Paediatrician who shared my concerns. Milo was still in the NICU and he had not yet opened his eyes. He mentioned that his hair and skin tone was a concern, now Milo did have jaundice, so he was a little yellow but still very pale. The Doctor organised for an Ophthalmologist to come and see Milo in a couple of days to check his eyes.

At five days old an Ophthalmologist came to assess Milo. It was a very bittersweet moment. He was very cold and blunt with how he confirmed it was Albinism saying, 'yes he is blind due to Albinism'. He then looked at Milo's Dad and asked 'do you have it?' Being much darker skinned and with very brown eyes we both looked confused but he looked in his eyes saying no but you have features. He then said protect his skin and eyes and I will see you in the clinic in three months and walked away. Milo's Dad and I sat shocked, crying while cuddling our baby not knowing what to do or where to go. A nurse came over to do Milo's checks and saw our upset faces. She asked if we understood what was said and if we had any questions which of course we did. But even the Doctor on that day admitted that as Albinism is rare he does not know much about it. So, he would make some calls to get us some information. We then had to leave our baby in the NICU not fully knowing what this meant for him and Doctors telling us they did not know much about the condition.

That night neither of us could sleep. I was still in the hospital and Milo's Dad was at home. He found an organisation called The Albinism Fellowship. The person he spoke to gave more positive information and practical advice, like we need to ensure Milo was referred to a Dermatologist for his skin as we need to ensure we keep his skin protected, not just in the summer months but all year round. He will have light sensitive eyes and not just sunlight but some indoor lighting. Milo has Nystagmus with his Albinism and we were told to expect to see some movement in his eyes soon. By six weeks old we began to see his eye moving from left to right and up and down.

For the next three months we pretty much lived in darkness with sheets up at the window blocking light coming in during the day. Most days he didn't open his eyes until the evening time. Every time I took him out I was petrified of his skin burning. At this stage his eyes still looked very red. We got lots of comments from people. Some days while shopping I'd put a hat on him and cover him over as I could not cope with the comments and questions.

I remember once taking my eldest daughter Alice to the local library and I was carrying Milo, a lady approached us and said 'his hair is so fair he could be an albino' before I could answer, my then nine year old looked at this lady and said 'that is because he is albino but you say a person with Albinism otherwise it's rude'. The lady looked at me and laughed. I looked her in the eye and said 'yep what she said' and we then walked away. This is not an isolated event, every day Milo gets comments about his hair and eyes. We hear things like:

I don't mean to be rude but...

Do you dye his hair?

Do you know his hair will get darker,

my son was blonde now he has brown hair!

Does he have red eyes?

What's his life expectancy?

Well, he can't be blind he wears glasses.

The first year was hard, no it was more than hard it was hell. There were so many appointments and so many Doctors who knew less than us about Albinism. One even Googled it during an appointment. It was then we requested a second opinion. I also went to counselling as my anxiety was through the roof. Milo had and still has very poor sleep. Having expected to have a little olive-skinned dark-haired baby like his Daddy to have this baby with pure white hair and that was legally blind it felt like I was going through a grieving process for the baby I expected to have. I felt very isolated. I often had to cancel plans with friends as I knew Milo would not cope with what was planned or we had not slept so the day was shit before it had even started. I also gave up work to care for Milo as my job was in early years and I had worked with many children with special needs. I felt that I could give him the best being with him, plus I was petrified leaving him with anyone. But this was one of the best decisions I made.

I did not know if Milo could see or what he could see, although he smiled and laughed he would look past us or to the side. He was around six months the first time he reached out and touched my face then smiled at me. A truly magical moment I will never forget.

I began an Instagram page to try and find other families to see if this helped with my anxiety and I happened to find some of the most amazing people. People who I pretty much talk to daily. Most of us have had very similar experiences with the diagnosis process. Originally there were five of us in our little group. We now have over 30 members. One thing that comes out of this group is we often know more than the medical professionals.

When Milo reached two, I decided it was time for me to return to work, although we were told he would be developmentally delayed he was doing well. He had a slight speech and language delay but I had expected that due to his low vision. So, the process of picking childcare started. Due to my career being in childcare I was very particular and chose a preschool where I used to work. He was given the most amazing Key person called Marian who is still a huge part of our life. Just as he began to settle in COVID hit. But this did mean I got some extra time off with him and was able to work on his speech development.

By the September when he went back to preschool his speech was amazing, I always tried to give a commentary when talking to him. Making sure I label colours, shapes, size, ensuring I tell him when to step up and down. This helped him being in new environments and he was able to manoeuvre his way with familiar adults directing him which the preschool took on amazingly. They also never changed the room around so he could find things, every day when he arrived, they would walk him around the room showing him where everything was. This level of support ensured Milo thrived at preschool after being told that he would likely not need or even get an Educational Health Care Plan (EHCP). I knew I'd have a fight on my hands.

First things first, the dreaded search for a school. I had one I knew I wanted to consider but we lived out of the catchment area, but my daughter went there and I knew they were amazing with children with SEND and learning differences. As I was told Milo might not actually qualify for an EHCP, I knew they would be able to meet his needs in the interim and help apply again for an EHCP. To throw a spanner in the works our QTVI suggested we meet with our local Vision Impairment school, which is a hub for the county. The school had agreed they could meet Milo's needs, but he would need that EHCP, but they did have a space in their nursery and did Milo want a space. I shouted YES!! But I then remembered that I needed to take Milo to see the school first and I am glad I did. The environment was just not for him or me, I didn't get that feeling that he belonged there. So, I took him to my daughter's old school and yes that was for him. The environment, the way the adults engaged with him, the outside area, it just felt right. Next step was pushing for this EHCP!

Writing Milo's EHCP was a very emotionally draining experience for me. I have written many of these in a professional capacity but never as a mum. It took me six weeks to complete the assessment request. I spent time talking to the Guide Dogs Education support team and the RNIB looking at the VI curriculum. One of the hardest things of this is not actually knowing what is going to be beneficial to Milo, what he will prefer to use. His vision is his and I feel it important that he has experiences with all the technologies and equipment that's available so he can choose what works for him, so I put them all in his request. I outlined how these formative years will impact on how he learns later in his education and being able to explore all these methods of learning will ensure that he can thrive, just like his peers. We got it and got a high funding band too.

The issue I find with Milo is he is not blind enough to be 'special needs' but he is not 'typical' enough to be the same as his peers, so he sits in limbo. Although he is severely sight impaired meaning he is legally blind, because he 'copes' well, a term I hate, his needs are often overlooked. I have had to fight for him to learn braille and touch typing as these will make daily life at school easier for him, it will mean he is able to learn at the same pace as his peers. However, the Local Authority feel this is not necessary until he is struggling, which boggles my mind. So, I ensured it was in his EHCP outcome and we do any prep for this at home and share resources with his teacher who fully embraces him learning anything and everything that will make his learning easier.

He has finished his first year in school and is developing as expected for a child of his age. Now this is due to adjustments the school has made for him. If they hadn't, he would not be doing so well. Year one will be the test for him but whatever happens I am so incredibly proud of him.

Helpful things I always share with parents just starting this journey are:

- Enjoy them- before you know it, they are running around bumping into things scaring the crap out of you.
- Find other families in the same situation, parents often know more than the medical professionals.
- Don't be afraid to ask questions or in fact ask for a second opinion.
- When you first get the diagnosis, don't feel you have to start telling everyone. Let it sit with you, find out information.
- It's okay to feel sad about it, it's okay for things to be hard, it's okay to be angry.
- Most importantly, be kind to yourself. Your feelings are valid and it does get easier if you find a new kind of perfect.

Layla Twinn

About the Author

Layla Twinn is a dedicated SENDCo with nearly 20 years of experience supporting children with SEND and learning differences. She became more passionate about advocating for SEND families after the birth of her first child.

In 2017, Layla proudly became a SEND mum to a little boy with Albinism. Her struggle to access support for her blind child fuelled her desire to speak louder, and fight harder for those who lack a voice, while breaking down stereotypes.

Chapter 3

A Spectrum Of Rainbows

Hannah Rose

O h shit... here we go again!

Teddy had previously met his milestones, he was walking on time, babbling, clapping, making eye contact. Then when he turned 16 months old, everything changed! The clapping turned into flapping, the babbling turned into 'eeeeing', the milestones became few and far between. He was going through a regression! I had an inkling that he was autistic at 9 months old because even though he was meeting milestones, something was telling me he was autistic. Everyone said I was just being dramatic, but mother knows best! 'He is a covid baby', 'boys are lazy', 'he is just copying his big sister', 'just let him be a baby, he will grow out if it'. How are comments like these going to help my little boy get the early intervention he needs? They are about as useful as decaffeinated coffee! They forget this is not my first rodeo, and this time I am feeling the complete opposite of what I did when we went through it with Teddys big sister Amelia! This time I felt love, joy, acceptance, happy, content and most of all proud, proud of how 3 years can change your outlook on this rollercoaster of a journey.

I knew Teddy was autistic! I did not need a professional to tell me he was but this time round, I wanted that diagnosis for him. Without it I could not fight for what he needs to thrive in life. This life is hard and even with an autism diagnosis things are not just handed to you on a plate.

I started the process when Teddy was 18 months old as we all know how long waiting lists are and early intervention is key right? Ha! If only there was such a thing as early intervention. Luckily for me I had a head start with what I went through with Amelia only a few years before. When I went through the diagnosis process with Amelia, I was very much in denial, and I went through a stage of grief for the life I thought we would have! I felt angry, scared, overwhelmed, jealous, defeated and so heartbroken. I didn't know what this meant for us and most importantly what this meant for Amelia. Her traits started right from the very beginning, there was no regression. She didn't meet any of her milestones; I was just so wrapped up in our perfect little family bubble that I couldn't see what was right in front of me, even if it high-fived me in the face with a chair.

Looking back at videos of when Amelia was little it was obvious; deep down I knew she was different, but I put my head in the sand and told everyone that tried to tell me otherwise that she will catch up. Back then I didn't want a diagnosis. I didn't want the 'label'. I wanted her to have the best chance in life and achieve remarkable things. I was completely oblivious to the arm flapping, spinning, not answering to her name, the no eye contact, no awareness of people or surroundings, tapping every object in sight, fascination with lights, tiptoe walking, no interest in toys or role play, repetitive finger flicking, loud vocal stims, no awareness of danger, no speech, lined everything up. She hated noise unless she was the one making it. She would repeatedly listen to the most irritating 10 second clip on YouTube you could ever imagine, on full volume. She would become very fixated to certain wooden letters of the alphabet and if that letter ever got lost you could not just replace it, nope! She would know it was different. We would have to turn the house upside down, searching for hours whilst sweating like pigs, praying we would find it before all hell broke loose.

As the weeks passed by, Amelia's traits became more apparent and harder to turn a blind eye to. I had some very dark and emotional days whilst we started the process of getting Amelia a diagnosis. I felt like a failure. I questioned 'why us?'. Hadn't we been through enough with having 9 miscarriages? Were we being punished for something?

I found myself being envious of anyone that had a child that was developing typically. I got so angry at the parents that would take for granted the number of times their toddler called out to them. I was longing to hear her say 'mum'. I spent numerous nights crying myself to sleep wondering what the future holds. I felt useless, what did I know about how to raise a child with complex needs? I felt ashamed and guilty that I was not enjoying my time with Amelia, I had my head in books and online forums researching how to support her.

Soon after, we were given Amelia's diagnosis and the famous "green folder" full of leaflets and sent on our way. She was diagnosed with Autism, Global Developmental Delay, Sensory Processing Disorder and social and communication difficulties. No one can ever prepare you for how lonely you feel afterwards or the worry with having to protect your child from the world she has no awareness of. The feeling I had before the diagnosis was like the entire world was on my shoulders because I was trying to figure out how to navigate this new life without a map. Once we got that diagnosis, the feeling went from my shoulders to a crippling ache in my heart. I did not know what to do and had nowhere to turn. All I had was a pointless green folder and unconditional love for my beautiful girl.

When you have children, you think about things like what career might they have when they grow up? Will they go to university? Will they get married? Have kids? But when you have children with additional needs, the questions change. It is the uncertainty of the unknown. Will they be able to communicate? Would they have friends? Could they get a job? Are they going to be able to live independently? Will I need to live FOREVER? You want your children to be able to live a fulfilled life, but will they be able to?

With Teddy it was so very different. We had gone through so much before Ted came along, I was a completely different person. Not because of the books or the online forums but from living in the moment, entering Amelia's world. She taught me our new way of living, and it was beautiful. Our very own colourful wonderland! She has taught me more than I will ever be able to teach her! By the time things started with Teddy, Amelia was happy and settled in a specialist school and she was loving it.

Teddy's traits matched a lot of Amelia's. The tiptoe walking, the spinning, the no understanding of the world around him, not playing with toys, lined everything up and the eye contact and answering to his name became less after his regression. Amelia's hand flapping was like a graceful butterfly whereas Teddy's was more like a Jazz Hand flap. Their stims are one of my favourite parts about them!

Even with siblings it is clear that one size does not fit all. While there were similarities between Amelia and Teddy, like sensory issues, restricted diet, sleep difficulties and toilet training problems, their learning styles and how these challenges presented themselves required different approaches. For example, Amelia used PECS and Makaton. This worked well for her, and with the help of this she was able to communicate her wants and needs. She is now a walking talking PECS book and every sentence starts with "I want" no matter what she is going to say. I taught myself Makaton so I could help support Amelia more with her communication. It worked so well when Amelia had no speech as we found signs and symbols helped. Even though Amelia doesn't use Makaton much now, since her speech has come on a little, I still very much enjoyed being able to use

Makaton so I began to do videos of different songs that I signed and shared them on social media.

PECS was not the right method for Teddy. Teddy couldn't communicate his needs or wants, he still can't. But he could sing many nursery rhymes over and over again. He also quickly learnt to repeat many scenes he had watched on YouTube from a programme called Ms Rachel. She is a hero in our house! I first believed this was what's known as Echolalia. However, after doing a little research, I realized that Teddy was also a Gestalt Language Processor. This is where the child would learn language in chunks of scripts rather than single words. Parts of the scripts they learn are then mixed up and turned into self-generated sentences. For example, Teddy learnt the phase 'I want more swings' That did not mean he actually wanted to go on the swing, but he was then able to turn it into a sentence that he did want and said 'I want more tickles'.

Getting Teddy's diagnosis was a celebration! We had the key to open the door to the next hurdle and I was set to take on the world for him like I did for his sister. But this time I was ready; I was excited, and I was empowered and that is all thanks to my 2 beautiful children. They give me the strength to fight even when I don't feel strong.

We thought our family was complete. We were so thankful after so many losses to have 2 healthy rainbow babies that had opened our eyes to the most magical world, but life has a funny way of throwing in a curve ball every so often. With that, along came our littlest, Autumn. She was the piece of us that we did not know was missing. I watched and expected her to follow suit. Maybe she wouldn't meet milestones or maybe she would go through a regression. Either way, she was loved, and she was brilliant so whatever her future holds, let's do it. I watched like a hawk as time went by, but the milestones were met, the regression didn't happen. Babbles became words, words became sentences.

She was something new, something I didn't know how to parent. I knew autism parenting. I would even go as far as saying I am quite good at it but toddler parenting? Tantrums instead of meltdowns? Back chat instead of non-speaking? Role play instead of stimming? What is this newness? I feel like a first-time parent with a newborn baby again. She is now 2 and doing so well. She is super clever, and the sass is strong within her. She is her siblings' biggest fan and is learning Makaton to communicate with Amelia and Teddy. She is the most beautiful, caring and kind little girl and I am so proud of how she adapts to the world we know at such an early age.

I am fully aware that Autumn has to deal with a lot having 2 autistic siblings with extremely high and complex needs. I have my eyes wide open, and I will make sure that she will get just as much love and support as Amelia and Teddy does. Yes, that will look different. Her big brother and sister will have appointments and assessments and there will be places we cannot go because it will be too much for them, but that doesn't mean Autumn will miss out. We will make sure as a family she will get to do everything possible, even if that means we have to do it separately so they all get their own time with mum and dad to make memories doing what they enjoy, whatever that might be. Having children on the spectrum as well as having a neurotypical child can be challenging but it can also be exciting because each day holds a new adventure. Our life is perfectly complete, and my children make me a better parent every single day.

It's not easy, but with the support of my husband David, I can take on the world. A lot of people forget about the dads, they forget that they are on this journey too. They feel the same rollercoaster of emotions us mums do. When I first met David 15 years ago, he wasn't sure he even wanted kids, so to go from that to 3 children (2 with additional needs) is incredible and I will forever be thankful for the life we share together. Because of him I was able to give up my job to become a full-time parent carer and I will always be grateful for that.

Over the years I have learnt everything is a fight to get the right support all SEN children need, whether that is EHCP's, specialist provision, DLA, respite, the list goes on. I have also learnt that not everyone has your child's best interests at heart, even when they say they do (but that is another story for another time!)

My last message to other parents on this journey; getting that diagnosis for your child can be lonely, scary and an overwhelming ride of emotions. Those feelings are valid. It's OK! Allow yourself to process those feelings. Don't be hard on yourself. Once you have got all your emotions out and let go of everything you thought your child was going to be, you will feel empowered. You will embrace this new way of life and you will be ready to take on the world for your babies! At the end of the day, all we want for our children is the same thing that everybody wants for their kids; happiness and good health!

And finally, I would not be the person I am today without the love and support of my amazing mum and my 5 brothers and sisters. I watched my mum single-handedly bring up her children who are all neurodivergent one way or another and she did it without showing any weakness. I learnt from her that I do not crumble into pieces and that strength is something that you choose! I could not ask for a better family unit, no matter how little. It is important if you are on this journey to have a good support system. Whether that is your family, a handful of low-maintenance friends that understand if you cancel on them at the last minute, or a group of crazy mums that you met on social media who are navigating a similar path to you. It took me a while to find my people but now that I have, a new journey has begun.

Change will come and we will not stop until we get it!

Hannah Rose

About the Author

Hannah is a mum of 3 who once thought becoming a mum was an impossible dream. She has taught herself Makaton and now helps others learn on social media. Hannah is a founding member of SEND Reform England, campaigning for change to the very broken S.E.N.D education system.

Before having children Hannah studied performing arts and performed in many Theatres across the country. She then went on to be a Funstar Entertainer at Haven Holidays. Hannah met her husband, David, 15 years ago when she worked for Virgin Trains. She loves music and dancing around the kitchen to anything from pop to musicals! Hannah celebrates her rainbow babies every day and her love for her family shines through everything she does.

Chapter 4

Our Magical Mystery Tour Of Life

Sarah Williams

I remember the day like it was yesterday, when it truly hit me that Lillian was autistic, and my gut instinct was right.

I was sat on my front room floor with a lady from Portage (a service for pre-school SEND children and their families). She came to help me with intense interaction play to try to help Lillian with communication. This was April 2021 and Lillian was 2 years old. I remember she said, 'is there anything you want to ask me?' I said 'will I ever hear my little girl's voice? Is this all in my head? Others made me feel as if it was.' She said to me, 'it's very clear in my eyes that Lillian is on the higher end of the autistic spectrum and there is that chance you may never hear her voice, many autistic people don't talk or communicate like we do ever in their life.' The tears fell down my face, I had an awful feeling in my stomach, I couldn't talk or breathe. I was looking at Lillian thinking 'oh why my beautiful girl? Why us? How will I cope?' I didn't know what to do. All I wanted to do was call my dad, but I couldn't. Grief set in over the next few days. What if she wouldn't have the life I dreamed of for her? I didn't have the child I expected to have, I felt so alone. I pulled myself away from my friends as it was becoming obvious that Lillian was different, and I wasn't ready to be asked questions or talk about it yet. I was still coming to terms with the fact that Lillian was autistic myself.

Now, when looking back to 2020, I realise that I knew then that Lillie was different, but what it was that made her different I didn't know at the time. At first, I blamed Covid because we were locked away from the world for such a long time and I thought I'd wait and see. Now I can say I knew it wasn't that, but I think I was in denial. At first, my husband Reg would always tell me she was OK, and nothing was wrong but then when I started to look things up and say to him 'oh my god Lillian does this' he would agree. Then at about 10 months, we noticed Lillie would flap her hands and her feet would move in a circular motion. While doing this her full body would tense up and she was rigid. I was worried about this, so I started to look it up and came across SPD and stimming. This opened my eyes to a whole new world we were going to face together. Reg said, 'OK yeah, I can see it more now you say this.' I think he knew too but wanted to wait and see. I believe he was in denial until this point.

During 2021 I was struggling with my mental health. It was the darkest year of my life. On January 6th my dad was diagnosed with terminal lung cancer and only had months to live. My world came crashing down on me. I was going to lose my best friend, my first love, my dearest daddy. How would I carry on without him? Family members and I cared for my dad at home, where he wanted to spend his remaining time. It was definitely the hardest thing I've ever had to do in my life, watching someone you love deteriorate so fast in front of your eyes, knowing there's nothing you can do to help them. I left my family every day for five weeks from 7am until midnight or later most days. I felt I was failing my family because I wasn't fighting for Lillian. I couldn't at the time, I was a total mess. My dad only lasted 5 weeks with us and passed away peacefully at home on February 14th surrounded by his family. On this day of the year, hearts are meant to burst with love but mine was broken forever. That night I came home, didn't speak, went into the bath and cried for hours. I was grieving my dad and also knowing I needed to fight for Lillian. I couldn't cope. I didn't sleep or eat for weeks and weeks. I became depressed and unwell. After my dad's funeral, I was looking at pictures I took while he was poorly and a video of him smiling. I then remembered what he told me. 'My love I know I said she'll be alright, but you have to fight for her because no one else will and I know if anyone can do it you can.'

The support around having a child with a disability isn't great. I was struggling to get the help we needed as a family. I didn't know where to go or what to do to make sure Lillian had the right resources and the support she needed. In May 2021, I went to look at nurseries for her as I knew getting her into one meant that the professionals would notice that Lillie needed support and would help me with everything. Many said they wouldn't be able to meet Lillie's needs. I was heartbroken. It felt like as soon as I mentioned Lillian had complex needs and possible autism they didn't want to know, but I found a little charity run preschool that welcomed us with open arms. I explained all about Lillian and that I believed she would need an EHCP and constant supervision with a 1:1 support worker. From June 2021, I started to find myself again. I still felt broken, but I got up and spent time Googling everything I would need in place for Lillian. I pushed for all the medical professionals to listen to me and have Lillian tested for chromosomal disorders and for genetic testing to be carried out. I wanted everything to be checked so we knew what we were dealing with. There are many medical conditions in our family on both sides. They agreed to put her on the waiting list for this. Over the summer I wasn't coping with the stress of not knowing what Lillian's future looked like, but I knew preschool was coming up. She started in September 2021.

When Lillian first started preschool, it was so hard. I felt I put her into a school setting too early. She was only two years old, but I knew it was the right thing to do to get the ball rolling for her as early intervention is key. As the weeks went on, the staff said, 'yes we definitely agree with you and Lillian needs 1:1 and 2:1 support for her safety and all her needs.' They asked, 'do you want to start the process of applying for an EHCP?' My head hurt. I didn't really know what an EHCP was or where to even start with this. Lillie's preschool manager, Lyn helped show me what to do and I started it. We had many team meetings with many professionals, about Lillie and the support she needed. They all told me I didn't have enough evidence to start the EHCP yet and to wait till she was 4 years old. I said 'no! If you're not going to help me, I'll do it myself', and I did. It was stressful but I did it and the local authorities agreed and said Lillian would be assessed by an Educational Psychologist. This was done within a few weeks and with her report, the local authorities agreed again that Lillie would need a specialist school setting.

Now, this is where my big fight started. I took myself onto social media to find other families like us, to see if I could find support and help moving forward. I came across an account where a dad shared his journey about raising two autistic boys. (Stories about autism) I watched him and many others for weeks. I became a little obsessed with researching things I'd seen that fitted the profile Lillian showed. Then I thought I wanted to share our journey to connect with other families and help if I could. Mainly to share awareness about autistic people because I believe autism acceptance is so needed. James, from stories about autism, gave me the inspiration to set up our own account and I've never looked back. I called it littlemiss-happyfeet because Lillian is always up on her tiptoes, sprinkling happiness wherever she goes. I've come across so many other amazing accounts. I've learnt all about autism and sensory processing disorder and I've done speech and language courses. The autistic community on Instagram is just amazing, they just get it. They understand what it's like to walk in my shoes. We share so much content that helps and supports others, but at the same time we still struggle ourselves. We share most of that to help others on their journeys.

I started to share just our daily life at first, then when the time came, I shared about getting Lillian's specialist school placement. I was not expecting the fight that I had coming my way, then I learnt so many other families were experiencing this too. Not every child that needs an EHCP or a specialist schools place gets one. There aren't enough specialist schools. THERE ISN'T ENOUGH SUPPORT! I was offered a school place for Lillian twice and both times they pulled the chair from under me and said there wasn't the space, so she didn't have a place after all. I appealed against this and was taking it to tribunal. In the meantime, I went to my local papers about it all and set up a protest where I live in Plymouth, to let the local authorities know that I wasn't going anywhere. I wasn't giving up the fight and I would get my daughter the school place she needed. I would fight for every child out there that needed an EHCP or a specialist placement. Within a few weeks there was growing pressure on the local authorities, which I believe pushed them to finally secure a start date to begin building new classrooms for some of the specialist schools in my area. We were then offered a place at our chosen specialist school. I was over the moon. I cried so much because I never gave up, even when I wanted to. I knew no one else was going to fight for my daughter, so I had to. Even though Lillian had her school place, I didn't want to stop there; I wanted to help others.

That's when SEND Reform England began. I met other mums on Instagram and TikTok and we wanted to do something. We all have children with disabilities or complex needs so know how hard the fight was. The government needs to know things need to change. Things can't keep getting cut, more funding is needed for SEND education. The SEND education system is broken and we, along with the autistic community, want to change that. In just five weeks, we set up a petition and organised a protest in London. I was so anxious about this, to be fair all of the girls were. But we had to let the government know we were coming to make a stand because our children's world matters too. They deserve an education; they deserve to be treated as equals. Just because they were born different, doesn't mean they should get treated differently. I will remember that day in London for the rest of my life. I looked around at just how many people had come. There were so many of them and it wasn't even half of the people that wanted to be there. Knowing how many families are affected by the broken system they call SEND Education is truly heart-breaking, but we made a promise that we will not stop our fight until our voices are heard, until our children are seen and treated as equals and until the SEND education system has been reformed. I've found the fight for our children's rights so hard, but I'm hopeful that soon things may change.

This journey hasn't been the easiest. I've been so scared; I've been at a very low point and felt like giving up sometimes. I'm not embarrassed to admit we've had marriage problems at one stage as it's challenging, this way of life. We didn't expect this life and the shit that comes with it and at times it's damn hard. But we made it and together we face everything as a team. Reg is a very hands-on dad, he is an amazing daddy to all of our children, but Lillian is daddy's little princess.

As a mum of 5 children before Lillie, learning to parent all over again with a totally different approach has taught me so much. I'll never take the little things for granted again, we celebrate each and every little bit of progress Lillian makes. Lillian is now 4 years old, and we started this journey when she was just two. We have come so far. She is now starting to talk, and she amazes us each day. She is so clever and the funniest little girl. She may not have words, but she shows us she loves us every day. Lillian has taught me so much and has shown me a different way of parenting that I'll forever be grateful for because I thought our life was going to be full of sadness and difficulty.

If you're at the beginning of your journey, let me tell you something. It isn't always easy and you're going to have to fight like you've never had to before but if I could go back to the beginning and tell myself anything it would be, 'everything will be OK in the end.' You are going to gain the most beautifully different view of the world. I call it our magical mystery tour of life! Because each day is different, and you never know what it will bring.

I wish everyone could see how much joy Lillian brings us and how much she brightens our lives. I wouldn't change our life or Lillian for the world, but I will continue fighting to change the way the world views our Lillian.

TO BE CONTINUED...

Sarah Williams

About the Author

Sarah Williams, from Plymouth, is a mother of 6 children and leader/coordinator for S.E.N.D Reform England. Sarah is so passionate about advocating for her autistic daughter and supporting the SEN community because she knows how hard and lonely some days can be.

Sarah was diagnosed with ADHD at 16 but didn't find out about this diagnosis until she was 40 years old. Enjoy her story in this book and hold on because it's one hell of a rollercoaster of emotions!

Chapter 5

Everything Is Going To Be OK Mumma

Chelle Cox

'After observing Bobby today, I have no doubt he is autistic'

'Do you understand what that means?', 'Mrs Cox?'

'Michelle, Bobby is going to need a lot of help, possibly for the rest of his life'

That's when it finally hit me, this wasn't just a developmental delay, he wasn't going to catch up and he wasn't going to grow out of it. I felt my breathing shallow as I tried to push down the lump in my throat. Despite my best efforts, tears started to fill my eyes. The doctor reached out across the desk, put her hand over mine and said, 'I'm so sorry'. I just had to get out of there, I got to my feet and excused myself, leaving Gavin and Bobby behind. I found the nearest bathroom, locked myself in, sat down and just sobbed. My mind was racing with a million questions. Would he ever talk? Would he live independently? Who would take care of him if something happened to me and Gavin? I looked down at my hands and noticed they were subconsciously rubbing my huge bump. I reached into my pocket, pulled out my phone and googled 'is autism genetic?'

Back in the car, Gavin and I drove home in silence, both trying to digest what we'd been told. After about 10 minutes, I looked back at Bobby in his car seat. He stopped flicking his toy, looked me directly in the eye and gave me the biggest smile ever, as if to say, 'Everything is going to be ok mumma'. It was a lightbulb moment. Nothing had changed. Bobby was still Bobby, my wonderful, cheeky, gorgeous blue-eyed boy. The boy we fought so hard to have after years of infertility and then finally falling pregnant through IVF treatment. I'd be lying if I said that was the beginning and end of my own journey in acceptance of his diagnosis, but I just knew he was right, it was going to be OK. I knew that we'd do everything possible to get him the best help out there and give him the best life we possibly could.

Leading up to that day four years ago, a few people had casually mentioned autism and I had dismissed it completely. I wasn't in denial, I knew there was 'something', but autism? No, it couldn't be autism. Autism to me, was structure and order, lining up toys and no interest in social interaction. Autism was Rain Man. That was the complete opposite to my little Tasmanian Devil who could make a mess in an empty room and loved nothing more than tickles and cuddles. I'm embarrassed now at just how little I knew back then, but then again, why would I know? There was no autism in my family, I had no friends with autistic children, and to my knowledge I had never even met an autistic person. Friends and family had downplayed my fears over Bobby's development. Comments like 'boys are lazy', 'you baby him too much' and 'every child reaches milestones in their own time', made me feel like a paranoid first-time mum. I remember the exact moment I decided to trust my instincts and call the Health Visitor when Bobby was around 18 months old.

One of Gavin's friends had a little boy a couple of weeks older than Bobby and I had asked his wife to come to our house for a play date. As they got out of the car and walked up path an aeroplane flew overhead. This gorgeous little boy stopped in his tracks, looked up, pointed to the sky and announced proudly 'Mummy aeroplane'. I was a first time mum and I didn't really know what was 'normal' for a child this age. But watching the boys side by side, the difference between them was startling. Not only had Bobby not said any words, but he never seemed to notice things like this, he wasn't even pointing. After they left, I called the Health Visitor and arranged a visit. Fourteen months later and I was crying in the toilets at our local hospital after receiving an autism diagnosis.

I have heard people say it's like going through a grieving process when you have a child with a disability. And while now I feel guilty that I ever felt like this, in those early days, the feelings of denial, anger, bargaining and sadness were very real and I completely understand the comparison. I was heartbroken. I was heavily pregnant with Mickey and I was scared of what the future held. I doubted myself as a mum and questioned if I had the strength to cope with a child with a disability and a newborn. The paediatrician offered Bobby genetic testing which I refused. I said I didn't want him prodded and poked with needles, which was true, but I was also terrified of what the results would be. I couldn't even think about the possibility that I would have TWO disabled children. I just wanted to enjoy the last few months of my pregnancy and look forward to Mickey's arrival.

During that time before Mickey's birth, Google became my best friend and my worst enemy. I had no one to talk to, but I had this overwhelming desire to know everything I possibly could about autism. I even did an online diploma, it kind of became my special interest. I definitely took some wrong turns down the Google rabbit hole during that time though, at one point I even purchased extortionately over-priced vitamins that claimed to help with speech delay. But I was on my own journey of understanding and acceptance and however silly it sounds to me now, it was all part of my learning curve. I needed to go through the process to get to the other side. Mickey was born on 20th January 2020, six days before Bobby's third birthday, by elective c-section.

At that time, Bobby was struggling massively with his sleep and was having huge sensory difficulties and daily meltdowns. Adding a screaming newborn into the mix wasn't easy. By March, the pandemic hit and we went into lockdown. I had no support at all. Gavin was a key worker so I spent the days in survival mode, on no sleep and in a constant state of alert. I couldn't leave the boys alone together, even for a few minutes. Bobby was too heavy handed and didn't understand that Mickey needed to be handled with care.

One morning, I took my eye off the ball. Mickey was laying on the floor under his baby gym and Bobby was preoccupied playing with his toys. I ran upstairs to use the bathroom and then I heard the most blood curdling cries. I ran downstairs to find Bobby on top of Mickey, his teeth clamped down on his chubby leg. Bobby is a huge oral sensory seeker and biting has always been a huge problem. I managed to get him off by forcefully pulling open his jaw. I grabbed Mickey and tried desperately to comfort him, the angry purple bruise on his leg had already appeared. It was bad and looked so much worse on Mickey's perfect milky skin. Bobby was crying too, I don't know if I had hurt him when I pulled him off, if I had scared him by shouting or if he was just pissed that I had interrupted his fun. And then I was sobbing uncontrollably. 'Mummy is so, so sorry', 'It's all my fault ', 'I am sorry my babies'. I wanted to comfort them both, but I couldn't. I only had one set of arms. The guilt was all consuming. It wasn't Bobby's fault, he didn't understand and now Mickey had been hurt and I should have prevented it.

A couple of hours later, the doorbell rang, I scooped Mickey up and went to answer the door. It was the Health Visitor. In all the drama of the morning, I had completely forgotten she was coming. The moment I saw her, the tears started falling as I explained what had happened. And then the words that no mother wants to hear are. 'I'm really sorry Michelle, but I do have to report this to Children's Services'. That moment was without a doubt the lowest I have ever felt in my life. She tried to reassure me that it was just protocol and that she did not have any concerns over the boy's welfare, but I didn't hear any of that. In my post-natal, sleep deprived brain, she was saying I was a terrible mum and Social Services were going to take away my boys because I clearly wasn't capable of doing even the basics of keeping them safe. I had failed them both. She made the call in my living room while I pretended to make tea in the kitchen. I was physically shaking as I eaves dropped in on the call between two strangers who were judging my parenting. Thankfully no action was taken. But I never left the boys alone together again, well not until Mickey was much bigger and Bobby's biting phase had passed.

The next 12 months were tough. Bobby was attending a mainstream nursery that couldn't meet his needs. He was supposed to be in nursery school for 30 hours a week, but they reduced his timetable to 10 hours and even then, they would call me regularly to pick him up early. The EHCP process went relatively smoothly and he was on the waiting list for a specialist school. The wait was agonising and it was my first experience of feeling let down by the system. I was watching Mickey like a hawk for signs of autism. At first, he seemed to be developing typically, saying the odd word, responding to his name and following instructions. However, at around 14 months old, he had a regression and almost overnight he lost it all. I found this incredibly difficult. Bobby never had these skills to begin with so I didn't really miss them. It was like he just didn't progress developmentally beyond 6 months old. But for Mickey to have them and then lose them, it felt almost cruel. I had been given a glimpse of typical motherhood and it felt as though it had been snatched away from me. When he was 18 months old, I called the Health Visitor once again for a pre-assessment.

By the time Bobby got his place in a specialist school, I was in a much better place. I had started to post on Instagram and connected with a number of other mums with autistic children. Through them I learnt a lot, not only about autism, but about the support available. I then joined TikTok and met so many incredibly inspirational mothers of autistic children. Meeting these women got me through the most challenging time of my life. I wasn't alone anymore. I even started to help others, often talking to these strangers during the long nights awake with the boys.

By July 2022, we were not only accepting of the boy's autism, but we had embraced it fully. Mickey's diagnosis was in complete contrast to Bobby's. Gavin and I walked into the paediatrician's office armed with so much more knowledge, we knew he was autistic and we wanted that diagnosis in order to access the support we knew he would need. We now understood the endless acronyms that were alien to us the first time around. We talked confidently about EHCPs, SALT, OT and DLA and I actually felt relieved walking out of there with the validation of a diagnosis. It was the first huge hurdle overcome, but I knew that was just the beginning of our fight. This wasn't our first rodeo.

I genuinely don't know where I would be without Gavin's support throughout this. I have spoken to many women whose relationships haven't survived the early years of having children with SEN and I often think it's not necessarily the children's challenges that puts the most pressure on relationships, but the constant fighting against the system. This is what I have always found most difficult. Not only does it take up so much time and energy, but the emotional strain is at times unbearable. You become consumed by it all and it feels like your lives are on hold while you wait. Waiting for a diagnosis, waiting for an EHCP, waiting for a specialist school, waiting for financial support. Waiting. Waiting. Waiting. All the time your child is struggling, missing out, falling further and further behind and it seems so unfair. At the time of writing, Mickey has an EHCP, but he was rejected for a place in a SEN provision at his first provision panel and we are looking to go back to panel in the autumn of 2023. However, I feel much more confident this time round. Confident in my understanding of his needs and in challenging the Local Authority's decisions.

The most important lesson I have learnt over the last few years is to let go of all preconceived ideas about parenting. Having had my first child at 38 and my second at 41, I really thought I had all my shit together and I would be a perfect mum. I read every book when I was pregnant with Bobby, but life has a way of throwing you a curveball and there is so much about motherhood that is out of our control. I had planned a natural birth and I felt such a failure when Bobby was born via emergency c-section and refused to breastfeed. The pressure we are put under to be perfect is completely unrealistic and the boys have taught me that there is no size that fits all. We have stopped trying to force our neurodiverse boys into a neurotypical world and it feels so liberating. Gone are the dreams of Pinterest- worthy summers at Disney World and they have been replaced by endless days of blowing bubbles, trampolining, and getting the sprinkler out in the garden.

Don't get me wrong, there are still times when the boys are struggling when I have moments of sadness and even wish things were different. I can't think too far into the future because not being around for the boys in a world that doesn't fully understand or accept them is terrifying. But I certainly don't feel short-changed anymore. I feel incredibly privileged to be their mum and have a glimpse of the world through their eyes.

Looking back now to October 2019, what seemed like a tragedy at the time, has actually turned into the most wonderful journey. I have changed, my priorities have changed, and I think I am a better, more compassionate, caring and patient person for having had my wonderful boys. As corny as it sounds, I feel that my experience of motherhood is exactly what was always supposed to be. I am blown away daily at their strength, determination, and bravery. I am in awe of their tenacity and every single milestone, however small, is celebrated in our home.

I wish I could go back to that paediatrician appointment knowing what I know now. I'd ask her why she was 'sorry'. My boys are amazing, every single part of them. There's absolutely nothing to be sorry about.

Chelle Cox

About the Author

Chelle lives in Hertfordshire with her Arsenal-mad husband Gavin and two gorgeous boys, Bobby and Mickey, who are both autistic and have significant learning difficulties. She is a passionate campaigner for S.E.N.D Reform England, using her previous experience as a Project Manager in a lot of the campaign administration, such as building the website.

Chelle's compassion for people has earned her the nickname 'Mama Chelle', often being the voice of reason and a shoulder to cry on when anyone is having a tough time. If ever Chelle was to have any spare time, you'd probably find her at a gig reliving the Brit-pop days or pottering around at home listening to her first love, George Michael.

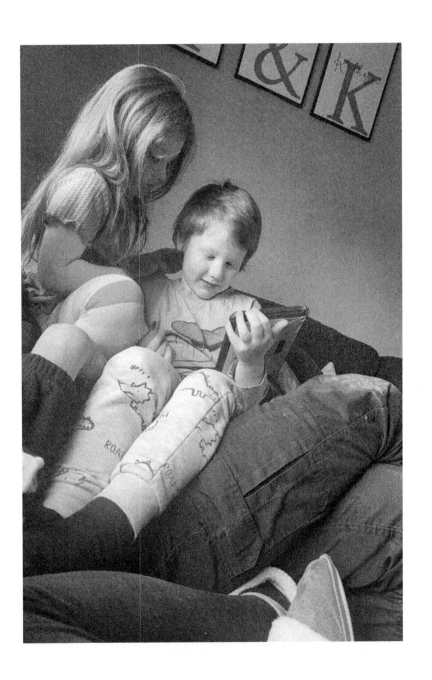

Chapter 6

Route Diverted

Kathryn Mulroy

It's a rainy Wednesday afternoon in October of 2018, our son Myles is about to turn two years old, I sat on the living room floor with my beautiful toddler trying to 'play' with him. I would often stare into space and wonder to myself 'why isn't he responding to any of my attempts to interact with him? Why is he just sitting, rocking back and forth flapping his hands?' I was already a mum to a nearly 8-year-old at that time, so I knew what Myles was 'supposed' to be doing development wise at age two, yet all developmental milestones (aside from physical ones) were nowhere in sight. Had I done something wrong? Was I not trying hard enough?

Little did I know what life had in store for us as a family.

I would learn in time that I actually knew very little.

Our daughter, Florrie, was born when Myles was 19 months old. Life was tough with two children under 2, as they say. When Florrie was new-born, we had the Health Visitor coming around to the house numerous times a week due to issues with her feeding. One Monday, as we were sitting with a brew on her usual visit for Florrie, she watched Myles for a good while. He was doing his little cute quirky flaps, now what I know to be stimming. A short space of time passed by and I wondered 'what is she staring at him for?!' She turned to me afterwards and said, 'Kathryn, I think we should be putting in some referrals.' I responded sharply with 'what for?' This was the very first time I would hear the sentence 'he's showing a lot of autistic traits'. It was said a lot more in the time following this and more professionals came to watch and observe him. I remember saying to my husband Tom after she had left, 'surely we would know if he's autistic? He has just got a speech delay!' Nothing more was said for a couple of weeks about it. My child wasn't autistic. I would have known, wouldn't I? This was the beginning of our journey, the beginning of what changed my whole way of thinking.

So it began; assessments, observations, more referrals. In this time, we found a nursery for him that had a brilliant reputation for children with additional needs. They too noticed, within a matter of a couple of weeks, that Myles was showing autistic traits. There we go; there's that sentence again! During this waiting time I threw myself into researching autism. I brought up a checklist on the internet one evening and that was the moment it fully sank in that these people were actually right. He ticked every single box, every single trait. Not long after this we had speech and language therapy, appointment after appointment. At the time, I didn't have a week where there wasn't somebody visiting the house or an appointment for Myles. I brought up, in conversation with the Speech Therapist, that sentence we kept hearing and I asked for her opinion. She explained her job was speech therapy but from getting to know Myles, yes he would be classed as 'a clear cut, black and white case', what did she mean? Very obviously autistic is what she meant.

The first consultant paediatrics appointment was very similar to the others. After yet more watching she sat us down and asked 'what do you think is the underlying cause of Myles' issues?' We explained that everyone was telling us autism. She responded with 'yes, I do believe so also.' From that moment on, we accepted this, we researched more, we found SEN baby play groups, we accepted our baby was a bit different than what we had anticipated. 9 months later Myles was formally diagnosed with autism spectrum disorder, a severe speech and language delay disorder and a condition called PICA. That day we cried a lot; we knew it was coming but why did it hurt so much? What was his life going to be like? We had so many questions and none of these were answered in the many leaflets we were given. It was so much to get our heads around.

During Myles' assessments, he had blood tests taken for any chromosomal defect disorders that could also be an underlying cause for some traits he showed. These all came back normal. I had a conversation with the Paediatrician about Florrie, 'does this mean she will also be autistic?' I was told it was unlikely due to the blood tests showing nothing genetically linked and also because she is a girl. In the next few months that followed I watched Florrie so closely, I had a list of so many traits now, I knew what I was looking for, right? She was developing typically for her age, talking in little sentences, answering to her name, following simple instructions; all things Myles didn't do. Tom used to tell me 'stop watching her Kathryn, she's fine, look she's talking', so I did.

Then when Florrie was 17 months old I noticed things changing. Her communication had disappeared, her words had gone, she stopped answering to her name, her eye contact changed to fleeting, she started spinning in circles, hand flapping; what on the earth was going on? My little girl was developing typically for her age but now it's all gone! How can a child just lose it all? My girl had effectively gone back in time. She was a 6-month old baby in her development, what is this? At her 2-year review with the Health Visitor she did all the same referrals as she did for Myles, saying she scores highly and the change in her is likely a huge regression; this is common in autism. I came home and it was going around my head, 'but this isn't the autism I have learnt about, this isn't the same as Myles.' I was so confused. Yet again, I had so many questions that nobody was answering. 'Just one of those things', I was told in regards to the regression. It wasn't though, it felt like a bomb had exploded in our lives. I was just getting my head around Myles' diagnosis and learning about his needs, then this bombshell! What more could I take...?

As Florrie's referrals went in during Covid, she wasn't seen as much as Myles and the waiting lists had increased so much since I went through it with him. Just under 2 years later, Florrie was formally diagnosed with autism spectrum disorder and severe speech and language delay disorder. The identical diagnosis to Myles, but how could they be so different? I now was a mum of 3 but 2 with additional needs. In the space of 2 years everything had changed. From that day forward, myself and Tom decided to learn everything we could to try to understand our children. They had no speech, how would they tell us things? I did courses on autism, asked questions at every appointment and learned everything I could. We also went through their echo process, another learning curve, and everything that came along with that. I said to Tom, 'Why is it this hard?' Not my children, but every single process we have to go through. Life was about to get harder.

We are now in the full swing of the summer holidays 2021, the summer between Myles finishing nursery and starting his specialist school placement. I was struggling mentally and physically. I was working night shifts in a job I loved, Tom was working day shifts. When we went to work opposites, all of our time was taken up with the children. I was trying to burn the candle at both ends, earn a living, have a career, be a mum and also a wife. Something had to give, I couldn't cope.

Myles' challenging behaviours at that time were so heightened. I was trying my best. Tom was trying his best. My friends and family, although very supportive, didn't understand the needs, or my children or what we were going through as a family. I would get asked to take them on play dates, but how do I go when my children don't know how to play? What if Myles lashes out at one of their children? No one understood and after a while they stopped asking. I had never felt so lonely and isolated as I did then. I had nobody to talk to, nobody understood. How could they? I tried reaching out for help from the services the Paediatrician had told me about at the diagnosis appointments. I called Social Services on myself. I was at a breaking point, covered in bruises from my then 4 year old son. I didn't know how to help him or myself. With nowhere to turn and nobody to turn to, to then be told 'your family doesn't meet the criteria.' I heard this a further 3 times when asking for support within Children's Complex Disability Social Care. Was our situation not deemed enough? I kept hearing the same sentences again. 'He's too young', 'things will improve', 'you are safeguarding them well', 'ask family to help you'.

Many evenings I sat on my landing floor pleading for some sleep, begging them to go back to sleep. Where was the help I was told about? Where were these services? Nowhere to be seen. We were left to struggle. I could feel myself slipping into this dark hole and I wasn't sure how I would get out of it.

One night Myles was awake at 2am as usual and I was scrolling on my phone, it was a TikTok video on Facebook. I had heard about TikTok, but I never really knew what it was. I downloaded it that week, I typed in autism and I found video after video of mums like me! Mums just talking about their children and talking about autism. They had so many comments from women who all felt the same! I closed off my phone and thought no more about it. A couple of weeks passed by. Myles started his school, things seemed to be getting better. I had some time to think for myself. I once again logged into TikTok, found loads more videos. I sat back and shouted 'they get it, maybe I could do a video!' But what would I talk about?

What better thing to talk about than autism and my family, eh?! This was the start. Suddenly I was making more videos and getting more comments from other desperate mums who felt like I did. Before long, I started speaking to mums and making friends with people who got it, people who understood everything I was saying. This led to talking to these women day and night when our kids were up in the middle of the night. I couldn't believe how my mood had changed just from making friends in our situation. Downloading TikTok on my landing that morning at 2am was one of the best decisions I've ever made. The support we all needed, it was there!

It's now 2023, Myles has been diagnosed over 4 years and Florrie 2 years. Things are good, things are better. We now have a Disability Social Worker after trying for so long. The children are happy and settled. I now know it's good to talk, but it's even better to talk to people who understand. I want to support other mums of children with SEND, give them that shoulder that I so badly needed a few years ago.

Kathryn Mulroy

About the Author

Kathryn is a mum of 3 and carer to her two youngest children. She admits to not having known much about autism to begin with but has learned so much, and truly embraces her children's differences.

Kathryn's experiences have led her to become a campaigner and advocate for the rights of SEND children and their families. She feels honoured to be able to share her story and is hopeful that it will reach those who need to hear that things will get better.

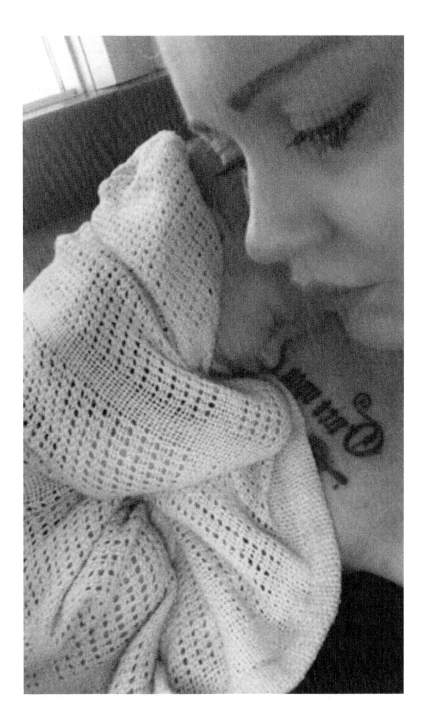

Chapter 7

When The Penny Drops

Kirsty Bailey

I locked my screen, laid my phone beside me and took a breath. The pins scratching my eyes and the boulder slowly dropping down my throat. As I felt the teardrop run down my face I knew. Tommy is autistic.

Now, I didn't diagnose Tommy because of TikTok. This is the thought process today. 'You saw a TikTok and diagnosed your child? Obviously you just wanted a label didn't you'. That's not how it works. What actually happened was myself, his dad, my entire family and all health professionals suspected he was autistic from the age of 9 months. As he grew and didn't progress mentally and became very repetitive in his body movements and missed every milestone. This was what made us believe he was autistic. But I'd never met an 18 month old autistic child so I had no visual. Just descriptions of traits. Like every time my older two children had a rash, and I hit Google to see different rashes. It helps to see what you are looking for. As I watched, over and over, this TikTok of an autistic child hand leading I realised 'this isn't a cute thing he's learned before he talks! This is his communication'.

I sat and cried for about an hour, completely lost in my own world. I could see every sign over the last 8 months flash past me. Every moment he didn't smile, every moment he shuddered at food, every scream when I tried to take him from the jumperoo, the fear of the spoon, the lack of acknowledgment when we entered the room. Every moment flashed.

By 12 months old he couldn't point or wave or clap. He hadn't developed a little knee bounce dance to music and in fact he wasn't walking around furniture. There was no trying to throw a ball and no turning pages in a book. In fact, he had missed 24 out of 30 milestones by the time he was at his 16 month check.

But what the Health Visitor was as concerned as me about was the regression. 'This does concern me. Children don't go backwards like this when they are learning'. She didn't need to tell me, I was well aware children don't just wake up one morning and have lost the ability to use a spoon or a cup. They don't wake up and lose the only word they have gained. They don't wake up silent. Not a sound, after being a child who randomly screamed and blew raspberries all day! Everyday! It just doesn't happen.

Even though, deep inside I knew, I guess at this point I was still holding out hope that the popular saying at the time 'he's a lockdown baby' was still true. That maybe he hadn't said bye to his nanny and grandad at the door so he never learned to wave. Maybe it was the lack of real world scenarios. Even though he had 2 cousins born just months apart who were doing all the things, he wasn't and he'd been in the same lockdown. Maybe, just maybe I hadn't coped in lockdown as well as I thought. So we made the decision to put Tommy in the nursery. One week after his first birthday we put him in for 3 hours a week to see how he got on out of the house, away from mummy and daddy and with trained early years staff. Even though I had the same training as them but maybe, just maybe I was being too 'mum!'

This encounter with an autistic child in a mainstream nursery would actually be so much more poignant in my journey. It would become my driving force to educate others and to later fight the system in Parliament. The coming months would shape my opinion on training in education, the lack of knowledge of autism, especially early signs of autism and of what can happen without the correct understanding of autism, how detrimental it can be.

We put Tommy in the Nursery for just 3 hours every Monday. This was from mid August until Christmas. A total of 17 weeks and he missed 2. The idea was he would attend 3 hours on a Monday morning, and we hoped, seeing other children, he would begin to copy from his peers. What we found was he ran up and down most of the time and if he wasn't running up and down, he just went to sleep. At that time of day he did not ever fall asleep on the other 6 days. I was paying £80 a month for him to sleep. But that was not the worst of it. On his second full day, when I collected Tommy, I rang the bell as usual. The baby room supervisor answered and then shot a horrified look across her face. She didn't lead me upstairs, she actually walked very quickly ahead of me. Not even holding the doors open for me. I picked up on this and sped up, ensuring I was only a split second away. As I entered the room she was frantically trying to unstrap a screaming Tommy from someone else's pram. Tommy was absolutely beside himself shaking and screaming.

In a split second I was told he had just woken, he had in fact been asleep for an hour and woken upset. I look back on this moment and absolutely hate myself for not saying more and even more now I know Tommy was absolutely in meltdown and they were understaffed for that situation. They had 3 non-walkers and 2 were babies. Tommy was a non-walker at 12 months old and having that sort of meltdown along with 2 crying 6 month old babies would have been unmanageable for the staff. It wasn't the right thing to do, restrain a screaming 12 month old, but being understaffed and undertrained to spot this, I see how it happened.

Tommy continued to just sleep every session for the next 12 weeks until we handed in his notice as Tommy had not progressed in a single area and pretty much slept for 1.5 hours of the 3 he was there. I was also coming closer and closer to realising Tommy was autistic. With every week it was clearer and clearer Tommy wasn't like other children. And in this period he also had his regression. We still wouldn't understand what that was for another 2 months. Until that TikTok video. When we handed in his nursery notice I felt like they were actually relieved. The response to my email simply read 'Oh no, not our Tommy. Ok I'll take your final payment from your deposit. Thank you'. Now, I wasn't expecting a fanfare, but I felt like they honestly read it and thought 'thank fuck'. I was a nursery nurse for 7 years. It's hard not to become attached to children, even if they aren't with you long, so to literally have that response honestly felt like he was a burden. The day he left we handed over Christmas and leaving gifts and his key worker literally acted like it was another day, not like she was saying goodbye to a child she had looked after for 4 months. Now, at 3 years old I still have zero trust in anyone to look after Tommy.

At this point, it was Christmas and Tommy had gone through his regression just 3 weeks prior, and we still had not really realised that this was what was happening. 6 weeks prior Tommy had been admitted to hospital with ulcers in his throat and a 39.5c temperature. When he then woke one morning completely silent, refusing food, not drinking from his beaker and tossing away his beloved dummy, we thought he had become ill again. After 10 days of eating nothing but watermelon we attended the doctors. She said she couldn't see anything but as you can imagine, Tommy made it hard to see inside his mouth. I remember literally saying, 'will it affect him long term if he's just eating watermelon?'. The doctor's response was through a 'don't be so stupid giggle' as she told me he will be fine in a few days. Again, let's fast forward another 18 months and Tommy's safe food is still watermelon and he still only eats around 10 foods. With food and regression being very obvious signs, I don't see why GPs don't have enough basic training to ask more questions when moments like this arrive. We weren't asked if by any chance does Tommy answer to his name or do you have any concerns about his development.

Our experience with doctors would, however, get better. Tommy's diagnosis process was relatively quick. I'm frequently told 'you're so lucky you got it so early'. I find this an utterly bizarre notion. Like I tricked the system or had an invite through the back door. The simple fact is, Tommy's traits are so prominent and obvious and he's so delayed that there is no way anyone would doubt he is autistic. It's that simple. His needs are so great that anyone can tell he is autistic in seconds. Does that make us lucky? Does it make us unlucky? It's just something we went through that's taken us on another path. It's just the day I heard the doctor say 'So, today I am going to give Thomas a diagnosis of autism spectrum disorder and speech delay disorder' and I actually just nodded. As you have probably come to realise. I knew anyway so this was just a formality. A diagnosis isn't what makes you autistic. It's being autistic that makes you autistic. Being handed the paperwork was just that. We had been very obviously living in this world with Tommy for a long time by this point. What came next also didn't surprise me!

As I write this it's been 4 months since his diagnosis. Tommy has only seen a Dietitian, who by the way was absolutely fabulous! I wish every professional had the training, experience and knowledge of autism she has. But it isn't the case and even then the wait times restrict us. She wanted to see Tommy again in a couple of months as he has had a significant weight drop. We could tell as he has gone back down from 6+ nappies to a size 5! It's a big weight drop. We received an appointment in the mail which has twice been pushed back. We are talking about a 3 year old not eating. Dropping weight! But still the appointment gets moved.

His Speech Therapist has refused to acknowledge Tommy's way of learning, continuing to treat him like a text book and offer only methods like 'withhold his drink from him until he speaks', owing to the fact around 30% of autistic individuals remain non verbal, Tommy could be waiting for a drink forever. I even called his Speech Therapist who advised that Tommy had been discussed at a panel for an EHCP. Apparently they agreed he met criteria and she said there would be another meeting that week and would call me back. That was 3 months ago and I've heard nothing! Even though she promised to call me with an update. How on earth can anyone put their faith in a professional who can't even make a phone call. Technically Tommy is supposed to have one hour a week with her but I said don't bother. So she should be able to allocate one phone call in 3 months.

Now, around 2 years into our journey, I have taken courses on sensory integration, feeding therapy and gestalt language processing. I've listened to podcast after podcast from Speech Therapists and built connections with, not only amazing therapists but mums across the community. I'm watching Tommy thrive because he has the right setting and understanding. I'm learning from life experiences, not just a 40 year old text book. We are in a world of sharing with social media and as a SEN mum, I don't know what I would do without it. Some days I have just the knowledge that my cuts on my face are from frustration or my bite marks from regulation are the norm in our world. I'm not alone in how I feel. What I'm experiencing. Other days I learn an amazing new strategy or game because someone shared.

Have I used social media as an outlet? A therapy? Absolutely! Am I grateful for that first TikTok? The one that made me accept Tommys autism? The one that led me to amazing friendships and a fight for a SEND Reform?

I wouldn't change a step!

Kirsty Bailey

About the Author

Kirsty Bailey is a business owner, content creator and mum of 3. She has an NVQ in early years development and has been working closely with some of the top speech and language and sensory integration trained therapists. Kirsty uses this knowledge to help other parents using social media platforms. Her passion is in speech therapy and helping fill the gap in services by advocating for change in therapy services.

Kirsty is also one of the founding members of SEND Reform England, a group set up to tackle the government failings and reform the system to help our children thrive. She is home schooling her 3-year-old autistic son.

Chapter 8

Learning To Ride The Wave

Siobhan Stephenson

L ooking down at the positive pregnancy test with a nervous feeling in my stomach, I said to myself 'I can't look after a baby, I can't even look after myself'. I had just turned 18 and recently passed army selection with a start date to begin basic training. I felt like my life was over, but little did 18-year-old me know that Frankie was going to be the best thing that ever happened to me.

Fast forward to Frankie's first birthday. He was the happiest boy and loved lining up his cars. Still no form of communication or words. The Health Visitor reassured me that this was completely normal for a child his age and not to worry. But I was still worried. As the months went by Frankie was not gaining any communication. He became seriously overwhelmed by noise and gained a sleep pattern of an owl. He refused to eat certain textured foods, and I started to tell myself. 'Maybe it's me'. I had comments from people telling me to 'read with him more' but Frankie wouldn't simply sit for long enough. 'He will eat when he's hungry', this wasn't the case. 'Have you tried sleep training?' This was probably the lowest moment on our journey because I felt like I was failing him.

Shortly before Frankie's 2nd birthday the Health Visitor came out to do his 2-year check. I had a dull feeling in my stomach because I knew something wasn't right. After she did her assessment, she told me not to worry but she was going to refer Frankie to the Paediatrician, and this is where our whole journey began.

Whist sat in the waiting room waiting to be called, I had so many thoughts. I was so scared, but we had only just begun this journey. After the Paediatrician did her assessments. She sat me down and said, 'I am pretty certain that Frankie has autism, we will refer him for further assessments'. 'Do you understand?' I replied yes. But deep down I didn't understand. I knew nothing about autism, there wasn't TikTok or many support groups online. I felt so alone all I could ask myself is why my child.

When Frankie turned 2 and a half, I decided that I would enrol him into a nursery so I could start a college course and to see if it would help improve Frankie's social skills. Which it didn't. Frankie spent a lot of his time at nursery sitting in a corner by himself lining up cars and spinning in circles. Which absolutely broke my heart. He refused to communicate with any of the children at the nursery, but he loved his key worker, and we were so blessed to have a supportive nursery.

After Frankie's assessments were finished, we had our last meeting with the Paediatrician. I sat down on the hard cold chair looking at my innocent boy, stimming. And she said I can confirm from our assessments we have diagnosed Frankie with autism, global developmental delay and sensory processing disorder. After just 10 months Frankie was diagnosed. She handed me some leaflets labelled autism and referred him to Occupational Therapy to help with his sensory issues. My heart just sank. I was scared for the future.

Shortly after getting Frankie's diagnosis, we had a severe house fire. It completely ruined our house. We were safe but homeless. This completely ruined the structure and routine we had in place for Frankie. All his favourite things were gone overnight. I vaguely remember tucking him into bed after being rescued by firefighters, broken, because things could've been so much worse. We were housed in a mum and baby unit. We went from living out of a home to living out of bags and I was broken. A couple of weeks passed, and I found out that I was pregnant with Ava-Mae. I felt like she was a rainbow after the massive storm we had just gone through. But in the back of my mind all I could think about was if I could cope with another child along with meeting Frankie's needs. Would Frankie cope with a new baby in the house? How would it affect his routine? I felt every emotion. But after the pain we recently went through, I felt extremely grateful that I had the privilege to have more children.

Over the next 6-12 months life was a complete blur. Struggling with a new diagnosis of Frankie's autism and struggling really bad with morning sickness which landed me in hospital. Also, a new PTSD diagnosis after the trauma from the house fire. There was honestly no light at the end of the tunnel. But it was time to apply for Frankie's EHCP. At this time Frankie was already in a very supportive nursery and the SENCo helped me with this process. Due to my PTSD, I cannot remember a lot. But I remember the process took just over a year to get accepted and everyone agreed that a SEN school would be the best setting for Frankie's needs. But due to the lengthy time the EHCP process took, we deferred Frankie's school placement for a year. However, we actually did go and view some mainstream schools, which Frankie came along to. But it was very clear he would never have coped in a mainstream setting.

I gave birth to Ava-Mae on the 22nd February 2017. She was beautiful and our family was complete. Little did I know the next couple of months were going to be the hardest I've ever experienced. Frankie coped well with the new addition to our family. He never acknowledged her for weeks, but he loved it when she cried. Ava-Mae had severe colic and she never settled at night. At this point I was lucky if Frankie was sleeping 2 hours a night. Doing this alone was hard. Money was tight. I was trying to build up our life from the house fire. There were a few occasions I found myself at the food bank. I was so embarrassed.

Fighting for support seemed to be a never-ending battle. I felt like Frankie was diagnosed and that was it. Nothing changed. Frankie was referred to Occupational Therapy due to his lack of danger awareness and sensory issues; this referral was declined with a reply of 'it's autism related so there's nothing we can do; we will send some activities to you in the post which might help'. He was also referred to a Dietician. Frankie's eating had always been bad but progressively got worse. He went 5 days with no food but because Frankie wasn't underweight 'there was no need to worry' and our referral got declined. I started to wonder how bad things have to get before someone gives my son the help he so desperately needs and over the years I found out.

We moved out of the mum and baby unit into our own home. About a year after this I met Matthew and Frankie adored him. Frankie never had a male role model. His biological dad was never consistent and pretty much stopped seeing him after he got his autism diagnosis. Our relationship moved very fast and 3 months into our relationship I found out that I was pregnant with Esme. Even though it was a surprise we were so happy a couple months before my due date.

On the 15th July 2018 I had Esme and she slotted in perfectly into our family. Frankie started his new SEN school the following September. I was so excited for him but nervous on how he would react to his new routine with school. His school was amazing and offered transitional visits, which made the transition a lot smoother for Frankie. They also started Frankie with PECS, but he refused to use these at home. Frankie is 10 now and still refuses to use them at home. But over the years we have found our own way of communicating. The school helped with contacting professionals with referrals and were accepted and I finally felt Frankie was getting the support he so desperately needed. Which was a relief.

As Frankie got older his lack of danger awareness got worse and he was seeking to escape the house. Unfortunately, he succeeded in his attempt to escape. Whilst I was cooking dinner, he unlocked the door and Ava-Mae followed him. I had to make the phone call no parent wants to make. I called 999 and the police came to my house and sent out 3 police cars. Frankie had actually taken himself and his sister to the local police station which was around the corner. He loved looking at the police cars as we walked to school. At this time, he also was obsessed with road signs of which there was a big one opposite. After this Occupational therapy helped house us into a more suitable home as our landlord was refusing to add additional locks to keep Frankie safe. His lack of danger awareness became so bad that we had to apply for a wheelchair to help keep him safe while we were out. As days out became really difficult.

Then Covid hit. Frankie became very violent; I think it was due to the lack of routine and structure. He became really violent towards Ava. There was an incident where Frankie bit Ava and a few months after that he pushed Ava down the stairs. I really felt like I had to split myself in two keeping Ava safe. The school did a referral to Social Services and requested for a Disability Social Worker. After 4 referrals it was finally accepted, and they did a carers assessment where we were allocated 4 hours a week respite.

Frankie was referred to CAMHS as at this point, he was really struggling with his sleep and behaviour. In the beginning we had an amazing community nurse for Frankie. She did more in the year she was involved than they have done in the past 4 years. Frankie went to a sleep and behaviour clinic which really helped with his sleep. He is in a better sleep routine now. Not amazing but we were now getting a manageable amount of sleep. However, Frankie has been waiting for a learning disability assessment for over 3 years now.

I had been working with the school for just over a year on trying to get Frankie toilet trained. We were mainly working on getting him used to sitting on the toilet. So, during lockdown I decided as we were stuck in the house to toilet train him. Which we managed and to this day I am so proud of him. After 2 weeks of intensive toilet training Frankie was out of nappies!

When I fell pregnant with Ava-Mae I was always worried that she might have the struggles that Frankie did. However, she typically developed fine. She was a little chatterbox. Her favourite word was 'hiya'. But when she turned 18 months old, she regressed. All the words she knew she never said again. Ava-Mae was a very unsettled baby and toddler. She was always upset, and I found myself with a child attached to my hip 24/7. Ava-Mae was nonverbal up until she was 3. I went to the GP with my worries, and they referred her to the Paediatrician. All I could think of in the back of my head is 'oh no here we go again'. But never did I realise what fight we were up against.

The nursery referred Ava-Mae to speech and language where they did their assessments, but she was discharged, and I was told that she would catch up in her own time. I never had a good experience with speech and language as they discharged Frankie due to his lack of communication which completely baffled me and made me realise how flawed these services were.

After experiencing a quick diagnosis with Frankie. I was hoping the same would be for Ava-Mae. But how wrong was I. Ava-Mae was referred when she was 2 and a half years old and seen by the Paediatrician when she was 4. She was referred for autism assessments when she was 6 in June 2023. By this time Ava-Mae had started school. She slowly became verbal. However, she still very much struggles academically. She was a massive masker and the behaviours I was seeing at home the school wasn't seeing. I think that this is the hardest thing because no one believes you. The result of Ava-Mae's panel meeting was that she does not meet the criteria for an autism diagnosis. She was very close to getting one but due to the masking at school they couldn't give one. They need Ava-Mae to start struggling and unmasking in school before she will receive a diagnosis. So, in November 2024 Ava will be reassessed. They also feel like Ava meets the

ADHD criteria too which she will also be assessed for. They are hoping by that time Ava-Mae does start unmasking. But what if she doesn't? What about early intervention? Or doesn't this apply to the children that mask.

After I realised Ava-Mae might be autistic I did my own research and it made me realise things about myself. I am undiagnosed and currently on a 5-year waiting list for a diagnosis and will never want my daughter to go undiagnosed her whole life.

During this process I was so alone. But I decided to make a TikTok account to document our journey. If I felt alone then I can bet there were loads of other parents in the same boat as me. Of course, there were! I've made lots of friends for life and realised I'm not alone on this journey and I am so grateful. I wish I had this support network years ago as it definitely would've made the process a lot more bearable. We are now campaigning as SEND reform for the government to change the education system for children with educational health care needs. As much as I loved posting autism content I did unfortunately stop because with social media comes a lot of hate. I made the decision to keep my children off my TikTok platform.

Frankie is now 10 and he is thriving. He is in his last year of primary school, and I couldn't be more proud of him. We will continue to fight for Ava-Mae's diagnosis and for more support in school.

Life doesn't always go as planned. I have realised, on this journey, you just need to ride the wave and learn how to surf. As much as this journey has been hard, I wouldn't change it for the world.

Siobhan Stephenson

About the Author

Siobhan Stephenson is a 29-year-old campaigner for SEND Reform England and devoted mother of 3. Her eldest, Frankie, is autistic and attends a specialist provision. Ava-Mae, Siobhan's middle child, is currently awaiting assessment and her youngest, Esme, has no diagnosis.

Siobhan is honest about the obstacles she has had to overcome and the difficulty of her journey. She is also honest about sometimes hiding in her cupboard with a snack just to get 5 minutes of peace!

Chapter 9

Rebuilding The Village

George Davies

'Your son's not deaf, he can hear every word you're saying, he just doesn't understand you.'

Those words changed my life forever and I remember that moment with frightening clarity. The audiologist holding my hand, the sinking feeling in my stomach, my grip tightening on my son as he sat on my lap. My son didn't know his own name, he didn't speak or babble and in a haze of ignorance and denial I'd convinced myself he was deaf, I even hoped he was. Admitting that to myself now fills me with shame, how could any mother ever think that? But I did. Deafness felt tangible. Dare I say, even socially acceptable. The words 'autistic' and 'learning difficulties' terrified me and laid my own ignorance bare. It took me far longer to forgive myself for those emotions than it ever did to accept my son.

In the months that followed I spent every moment not with my kids, reading. I convinced myself that knowing everything would make me the mother my son deserved. If I hadn't already lost myself to motherhood, I sure as hell did then. Yet most nights I went to bed feeling like a failure.

Motherhood had felt so easy with my eldest son. Henry was the happiest baby. He loved the world, ate everything I gave him and hit all of his milestones bang on time. I was young and, I'll admit, a little bit smug. I convinced myself that every amazing thing he did was because I was such an amazing mother. So when Jonah arrived 23 months later I was super confident, maybe even arrogant. But as the saying goes, you never get 2 the same. Looking back now I can see the differences so clearly, the signs that were so glaringly obvious and yet I was in complete denial that Jonah was different, convincing myself he didn't love me and I was actually the worst mother in the world. Everyone around me blamed everything else you could imagine; 'he's just a colicky baby', 'he's just fussy', 'it's because he's your second', 'boys will be boys'. The list was endless. I knew deep in my soul he was different, it just took my heart a little while to catch up.

Three months after the hearing test we were back in the hospital, but this time for the first of many appointments with Jonah's paediatrician. He told me he believed Jonah was autistic and by then I knew he was. I wasn't the same woman that had sat broken at a hearing test months before. I was laser focused on one thing; making my boy's life the best it could be. Everything I had read said how important early intervention is, so that's what my son would get. I was so focused that I barely noticed the friends slipping away, the distance between my husband and I that had deepened into a chasm and, in truth, I didn't care. All that mattered was my 2 beautiful boys.

In the months that followed, the appointments and assessments were constant. They became my whole life. Jonah's formal diagnosis came two days before my 30th birthday, when he was 2 years and 4 months. I cried with relief. I had been holding my breath for a year and could finally breathe again. I wasn't scared or upset, just relieved. I wasn't crazy, I hadn't imagined it. My boy was different. I was so relieved that almost a whole year of analysing and being forced to talk non-stop to professionals about what my son couldn't do or struggled with, was over. I just wanted to be a mum, to enjoy my boys and celebrate all the magical things that make them who they are.

The hearing test had marked the beginning of an incredibly hard time and my first real step out of the other side of that came on a windy day. As I stood in the kitchen cleaning, Jonah in and out of the garden I heard the most beautiful belly laughs. I assumed it was Henry making his brother laugh but as I looked out Jonah was sat alone. At first glance, he appeared to be laughing at nothing. I crept quietly outside, desperate to see what was making him so happy, only to be left confused. Eventually I saw it. The wind. The wind was making a teeny shrub I'd planted wobble and my boy was enchanted. Holding his breath in anticipation, and then roaring with laughter every time the wind made the shrub dance. It was so simple and so powerful. My boy, who couldn't speak and struggled to engage with people and the world, saw beauty where most of us wouldn't have even noticed. The tears streamed down my face, not from sadness but from hope. My boy saw beauty in places I couldn't. I didn't need books or courses to learn about my son, all I needed was right in front of me. As I sat on the floor and shared his laughter, I knew everything would be OK.

I wasn't scared when my marriage inevitably ended. I had my boys and if that was all I ever had then that was enough. Becoming a parent changes you, discovering you're a SEND parent reveals you. It challenges you in ways that are hard to articulate but if you let it, it can be the making of you. Henry made me a mum, Jonah made us a family and they both showed me who I was and who I longed to be. But I'd be lying if I said I wasn't lonely. Loneliness would hit in the evenings when the boys went to bed and it was palpable. They say it takes a village to raise a child but I'd watched as my villagers moved gently away, unsure of what to say or how to include my wildly different little family. I didn't hate anyone for it, I let them go and cherished the best friend that loved my boys like her own and my mum, who would set the world on fire for her grandkids.

The loneliness ebbed away as our world, that had once felt so small, began to get bigger again as I watched Jonah start to connect with the world. As Jonah found his place in the world, I found love. I had no idea, as I was falling in love with Gaz, that I was falling for my son's future best friend and greatest protector, but suddenly there he was. I blurted out that my youngest son was autistic and had severe learning difficulties before we ever had a date and his response was simply 'is he happy?'. It took me by surprise because the common reaction is usually 'I'm sorry'. Two words that I think people mean with sympathy but they just hit wrong. I'm not sorry and Jonah is certainly not sorry, he is far too busy being unashamedly himself.

Having a child that is so wildly different is a gift. We can all be guilty of worrying too much about what other people think and I began to realise just how much of a people pleaser I had been. Finding ways into my son's world also led me back to finding and accepting who I was. If my boy wanted to vocally stim his way around a supermarket, why not? And if I wanted bright orange hair then why not that too? I realised I didn't want to force Jonah to fit into a world dominated by unspoken social norms, I wanted to change them. It wasn't just about letting go of the picture in my head of what I thought life would be, it was celebrating who we all are. In the beginning the stares had upset me so much and not just stares but filthy looks and negative comments. But as I evolved so did my attitude to them. I don't get upset anymore. Most of the time I don't even notice, but when I do, I feel sorry for those people. Anybody staring at or judging your child is certainly not living their best life, but we were.

Sensory play invaded my home, at one point we had a paddling pool full of shredded paper in our living room. Why? Because why the fuck not, it made my son happy. I stopped obsessing over his diet and celebrated every new food like a lottery win. I stopped fixating on missed milestones and instead started celebrating what I call 'the little big moments'. The moments most parents take for granted but for us feel like the world. I started actively seeking out other people that lived free because not all SEN parents are created equal. Some people are obsessed with the whys, cures or forcing their child to compromise their sense of self for the sake of fitting in but I got brave. When you like who you are, you aren't afraid to approach people. When it came to the first parent's meet and greet at Jonah's new school, I offered up my number to another mum and found an amazing woman who has since become a best friend. In the years since then, we have shared many wonderful times, such as sitting together, laughing with a glass of wine, whilst our boys emptied 10 bottles of bubble bath into a paddling pool and loved every minute of it.

I took to social media to share our life and hopefully make other mums feel less alone, and found a group of women that made my heart happy and reignited my passion for change. We've organised protests and petitions and continue to challenge government and society on how they see and treat our children. My village, that once felt so abandoned, is full of love, laughter and acceptance. It's not that life suddenly became easy, just that I got better at living it, better at finding the balance between being a SEN mum and being myself. I've accepted that time passes differently when you're a SEN mum. We live in seasons, not in the traditional sense but emotionally. Sometimes seasons can feel like winter, dark and oppressive, if Jonah's anxiety is high or he's displaying challenging behaviour, but I know summer will come. We will, as we always have, find a way.

Speech never came for Jonah. He is 12 now and classed as non-verbal or pre-verbal, depending on which you prefer. It was the hardest part to let go. We all assume we will be able to have conversations with our children and it's so deeply painful when you can't that it's hard to put into words. For years I cried the night before Jonah's birthday. I'd told myself 3 would the age he'd started talking, then 4, then 5, then 6. Letting go of that was, for me, the hardest thing but I realised along the way that talking wasn't so important. The most important thing was communication and that shift in mindset changed everything.

Jonah can say a few words. They come at home mostly, his safe place, and he even calls me Mum. But speech is a complicated thing, as he learns a new word, we lose an old one. Some words have only ever been uttered once, never to be heard again. But if you think non speaking means quiet you'd be dead wrong. That boy is quite possibly the loudest person I know! He babbles, sings songs only he knows and has specific noises for pretty much everything. I've heard people say they are their children's voice but for me, I'm a translator. I speak fluent Jonah and can help others learn his language too. We use photographs so Jonah can choose where he wants to go and his mental map is unreal. He knows the route to every place we go simply by which way we walk. He is without doubt one of the funniest people I know and those conversations I longed for do happen now, just in a very unconventional way.

Sometimes I wish I could go back in time and tell myself it would be OK, that this life is different but never less. But instead I'll tell you, it will all be OK! You will watch in amazement as the things you never thought possible come to life. Maybe not in the way you expect or at the time others experience it but that's OK because you get a lifetime of little big moments. Having a child with additional needs is not a tragedy, it doesn't mean they can't live a life that's full of beauty and love and you deserve that too. Villages can be rebuilt and those dark seasons never last forever.

George Davies
About the Author

George is a mum of 2 and step mum of 2 who is incredibly passionate about sharing the beauty of parenting and life lived differently. As a founding member of the campaign group SEND Reform England, George has organised protests and petitioned the government to enact changes to the education system, to give all children and young people an educational setting they can thrive in.

Outside of mum life and campaign work George loves movies, music and knitting. George believes that a simple life filled with love and laughter is the best life.

Chapter 10

Perfectly Penny
Lucy Marriott

N o one expects, after a relatively easy pregnancy, to be told their brand-new baby has a disability.

No one, when they plan their future with their child, dreams of endless appointments, meetings, and tests.

No one expects to have to fight for their child's right to an equal education.

Or to have to fight off bigger kids and teens and looks from parents, when you just want to use the one accessible swing in the whole park!

And yet here we are.

I'm Lucy. I had my first child (my biggest boy) 16 years ago then my second boy came along 2 years later. I did not expect to be having another child but after splitting with the boy's dad and meeting my person, Penny's dad, I realised there was room for one more.

When Penny was born, everything seemed as expected. For maybe 12 hours. I have a treasured picture of the moments after she was born, before we even had the words 'deaf' or 'disabled' in our minds. Where we thought, after a very difficult labour, that we were finally done with hospitals!

It all started with her ears. Penny didn't clear the first newborn hearing screening. (We do not say that she failed the hearing test because it puts negative connotations onto being deaf from the very start. In fact, I like to say she passed the deaf test!). She also didn't clear the second test. Or the third. After finally leaving the hospital, we were told that we needed to go back in a few days for more in depth testing, and I was distraught. Not at the prospect of my daughter being deaf but at the thought of having to step foot in that hospital again!

The phrase that was constantly repeated was 'it's probably just fluid'. It was like they were scared to say the word 'deaf' to us, and so we had a leaflet that explained in a nutshell the 'not fluid' outcome. After many, MANY more in-depth hearing assessments we found out that Penny had bilateral (both ears) moderate-severe (deafness is a spectrum) sensorineural (permanent) hearing loss. In other words, she's deaf, and would benefit from using hearing aids, which she would get when she was 8-10 weeks old.

Hearing tests on babies are a work of art. They must be asleep for the whole test for starters. Penny had patches of skin exfoliated to make it easier to attach sticky pads that recorded the brainwaves and reactions from the sounds being played via in the ear headphones. I spent many hours with my finger in Penny's mouth, as this was the only way to keep her soothed and asleep, the other hand was holding the earphones in her tiny ears, desperately trying to not move or make a sound for approximately 1.5 hours so that the Audiologist could get all the readings needed. Oh, and Penny was barely a week old when these tests started.

We really hit the ground running! After being told about the hearing aids, I panicked. I'd never even seen a hearing aid up close let alone having to learn how to use one on a tiny squirmy baby! Penny was pretty much the first deaf person I met, which is actually how it is for most hearing parents to deaf children. It's crazy to learn that around 90% of deaf children are born to hearing parents. And yet we know nothing of the deaf world beforehand!

On the back of this we were sent for many other tests including an MRI and blood tests. The Drs needed to know why Penny was, well, Penny! MRIs on babies require a general anaesthetic, apparently, they can't help but wriggle about, who knew?! Having to see my then 6-month-old be put under and then just leave her with the Drs was painful! Thankfully it was over pretty quickly, and I could hear her cries from the bottom of the corridor and I raced down to greet her with her favourite dummy and taggie!

We then found out from the MRI, she had abnormalities in the structure of her brain, the impact of which is still a 'wait and see' sort of thing, and her cochlear isn't fully formed. This possibly means she has something called EVA (enlarged vestibular aqueducts) which means she could lose the residual hearing she does have and will drop too profoundly deaf. I say 'possibly' because she requires a CT scan to be able to properly diagnose EVA (it wasn't clear on the MRIs), but as Penny now has a lot of anxiety in a medical setting due to some trauma, we are waiting until she's much older to put her through that, in the hope it'll be less stressful for her.

At 8-10 weeks of age, we were given her teeny tiny hearing aids, shown how to work them, given a bag of equipment and booklets and assigned a Teacher of the Deaf (TOD). In the early days we saw our TOD regularly, she went into more depth as to how to maintain the hearing aids, how to encourage communication with my baby, how to focus on speech (I also, despite being told she wouldn't 'need' sign language, decided to learn some basic signs to use alongside speech)

Hearing aids are expected to be worn 'all waking hours' which anyone with a small hearing aid wearing baby will tell you is almost impossible.

There was so much to learn as well as learning who my newborn was and all her quirks and preferences, which, with Penny, was quite the education. When they say no two babies are the same, THEY ARE CORRECT. Penny was my third, but I felt like a first-time mum all over again. It was the start of what would be a lifelong education on all things Penny.

So far we know she has a wobbly walk and limited mobility due to her brain differences and also hypermobility. She has also developed some minor tics (blinking, sniffing, 'hmm'-ing) and has an intention tremor, meaning when she tries to do something 'with intention' (such as writing, building blocks, putting a bubble wand back into the tube) she has a tremor that makes it tricky. We also suspect she is autistic, but we are still going through assessments. She also has other soft genetic markers that indicate a genetic thing going on, but the jury is still out in that.

It's been quite the journey and it hasn't always been easy by any means.

I felt the need to grieve. Grieve for the life I thought I was going to have. Grieve the child I thought I was going to have. It doesn't mean I love Penny any less, she's one of the loves of my life, but I think it's important to be permitted to feel that grief and process it. Without guilt.

Day to day we deal with hearing devices, work on communication using sign as well as speech, helping her get around, assisting her with fiddly things that her tremor makes more difficult, we try to avoid meltdowns from sensory overload or some other reason that we still can't explain. Penny relies on a rigid routine so when I know there's going to be a change (if there's any warning) I make sure Penny is aware of what's happening and why and deal with whatever reaction she has.

We are regularly at the Audiologist, having repeat hearing tests, which are much easier now she's older (as long as she's in the right frame of mind for it!) and she regularly needs new ear moulds. It's shocking how fast tiny ears grow! We have to prepare her for everything using visuals and making sure we are explaining things in a way she can understand. I've had to fund my own BSL courses in order to be able to fully communicate with my child. I've had to fight for a mobility pushchair so I can get her to school.

But aside from her diagnoses and the day-to-day work that goes on, Penny is a sassy, funny, too clever for her own good, beautiful beast of a 5 year old. She is exactly who she is meant to be.

She is perfectly Penny.

The obstacles we have are those put in place by society and the systems that should be working with us to allow our children to thrive in any environment. Going out causes me stress and anxiety, mostly due to other people. They stare, they whisper (some say things out loud assuming we are also deaf) They question, they are ignorant or just clueless. No one seems to think a child could be disabled.

Accessibility is also an issue. Places designed for kids are rarely designed for disabled kids. People just don't seem to think kids with disabilities exist. Like its only adults that are affected. So, finding accessible parks isn't fun! Every trip out has to be planned, researched, prepared for, so Penny knows what to expect, then we still have to be on guard knowing that something could go wrong, or Penny could have some kind of problem that we hadn't thought about. Nursery and school require a lot of preparation also, with endless meetings with teachers, SENDCos and our Teacher of the deaf, who also provides training to Penny's teachers throughout the school year. We make sure they are teaching Penny in a way that works for her, to ensure she can thrive as much as her non-disabled peers.

I am learning as we go as Penny's needs change as she grows, and as new things come up, more meetings are needed, and adjustments made to any care plans that are in place. It can be exhausting, always assessing and monitoring and adjusting.

Something that would make our life easier would be for other parents to educate themselves and their kids on kids like mine. Learning about disabled kids isn't just for the parents of disabled kids! If Penny's peers and other kids around her already had a basic understanding of inclusion and how certain things (like accessible swings) are put in place for kids like mine, a simple trip to the park for example, wouldn't be so anxiety-inducing. I will never stop fighting for Penny's right to inclusion and accessibility, I just wish the fight wasn't so relentless!

Lucy Marriott

About the Author

Lucy is a full time stay at home parent, after leaving her job in administration when her daughter was born 5 years ago. She doesn't have any fancy qualifications but she has 16 years of experience in being a mum to kids with additional needs.

Lucy advocates for inclusion and better understanding of kids with disabilities by those who have kids without disabilities. She fights endlessly to make sure each of her kids, with their varying additional needs, have the best chance in their education and life.

This chapter is dedicated to my wonderful, book loving mum, Tracy Urwin-Mann. The kind, brave, unwaveringly loving example she set, helped me to become a mother, and a woman, I can be proud of.

Chapter 11

A Mother's Instinct Never Fails

Sandeep Bains

I remember cradling Kavi in my arms whilst kissing him on his head, telling him repeatedly how much I loved him. I didn't want to put him down, we stayed snuggling for most of the night whilst I gazed at him in awe.

She believed she could, so she did (Scolding Wilder by R.S Grey).

I was exhausted from the days prior but I was running on sheer adrenaline and in disbelief of the beautiful life we had created. As soon as he entered the world he looked at me with those, now very familiar, puppy dog eyes, whilst his bottom lip quivered as he whimpered. He's always had the most beautiful sweet cry, even now at almost 7 years old. I finally understood and truly felt the meaning of a Mama Bear. I felt so overprotective of him as soon as I caught sight of him amongst the commotion of the hospital room. In that instant moment I felt like it was just me and him, in slow motion as I laid there in shock, reaching out for him, a connection like no other I had ever experienced.

Kavi's nature has always been very laid back and happy. I can't say that motherhood has been a breeze, but the good times definitely outweigh the hard. Weaning was an exceptionally hard time, and I have to be honest, it was not an enjoyable time for me. Whilst other mums would get excited, each day of weaning for me was filled with worry and anxiety. Kavi would struggle with textures and often gag or bring up full meals after he had finished them. After a few weeks he would stop opening his mouth for certain food groups - mainly vegetables (particularly anything green) and certain textures. The list of things he would eat just got shorter and shorter.

A memory I will always remember is sitting in a toddler sensory class watching all the other parents and children sitting in a circle with the group leader singing and signing 'say hello to the sun'. Kavi must have been about 18 months. He was the only one on the other side of the room playing with a toy, not interested in what was going on in the group session. I did wonder why it was only my toddler not interested but I also felt proud that he was his own person, he reminded me very much of myself when I was younger.

Although Autism had crossed my mind a lot of times before this, I could never be sure and would talk myself out of it. I would tick all the generic boxes on Google about whether my baby was autistic or not. I remember thinking he gave me eye contact even though it was fleeting (1-2 seconds) so he couldn't possibly be autistic. He was just speech delayed and knew what he wanted, that's all it was.

We would do different activities with Kavi throughout the day, and we found the more we did with him the less likely he would be to go to sleep. If we kept a calm environment for the second half of the day, it would be easier to get him down (easy meaning 2 hours instead of 5) but he would still struggle to fall asleep. I myself have never needed much sleep and have always struggled to switch off, so me and my husband used to joke that he had taken after me.

Being a first-time mum, I just thought that was part of his personality and he would grow out of it, as everyone kept telling me! I started to notice that he was different from his other peers at around 12 months old. If I would bring up with friends/family that I thought he could be autistic they would say I was being silly, and that he's too young; all babies develop in their own time. What I would have preferred them to say was 'I can tell you're worried, why don't you speak to the Health Visitor and see what they think, parents know best'.

When Kavi was about 2 and half, we were at a local birthday party. I remember having a conversation with one of the other mothers and a close friend of mine about the fact I thought he could be autistic. Kavi was eating his party food at this time but had spent the entire disco laid on the floor after being told off because he was trying to grab the disco lights off the DJ booth instead of listening to dance instructions from the entertainer. She turned around to look at him and mentioned that a close family member had an autistic child. She said that if he was autistic, he would be covering his ears and wouldn't be able to stand the noise and not to worry. I know she was saying this to put my mind at rest; her and every other person that had said similar.

What they didn't see was even though I would tick that Google tick box, I would obsessively be researching Autism the majority of nights or when I had a spare minute. I would read over the same information just to see if I had missed anything, or if anything had changed that day. I would go to sleep some nights thinking he can't be autistic, because he hadn't shown many traits that day, but then the next night I could be back to researching because a lot of the traits seemed to be there.

During this time Kavi was also suffering from repeat ear infections and high temperatures. He was poorly so often that we put him missing his milestones down to that.

The denial and clinging onto him not being autistic is now so loud and clear thinking back. When I go through all of his videos as a baby and see his big happy repetitive stims it's so obvious, but it wasn't at the time. I get so upset looking back through footage because all the traits were there, but we didn't want to see them.

Kavi had just turned 3 when lockdown hit. He was waiting to see an ENT Surgeon because Audiology suspected he had glue ear. We decided to have a private consultation with Dr Kelly who also worked for the NHS. During this consultation was the moment I knew Kavi was autistic, it was also confirmed that he did have glue ear. The surgeon's exact words were. 'The grommets could help Kavi 30% or 70%. He's signing his alphabet and counting to 100, he's just not communicating with you verbally. This would suggest to me that it's highly likely that he is on the Autistic Spectrum'. I was relieved, I hadn't been overthinking things, it wasn't all in my head. It didn't seem to faze me at that point, my true feelings would come later.

That very same day I rang Kavi's Paediatrician to have him referred for an Assessment. The Paediatrician had been trying to push me to have him referred for an Autism Assessment for a while but when we suspected he had glue ear we told ourselves that must be the reason he wasn't talking to us and that would explain everything. I also had a few friends whose children had thrived after having grommets inserted, so I was clinging onto the fact we would see the same for Kavi. Nothing much changed for Kavi speech wise, but the ear infections were less frequent, I was so glad. It was horrible seeing him so poorly all the time.

After Kavi had grommets inserted my husband was still very much in denial. We all have to get there in our own time. As each month passed my husband would say 'it's only been 1 month since he's had them fitted', 'it's only been 4 months since he had his grommets fitted'. This carried on until we were nearing 12 months since his op which is when he said 'Yeah, I think he's Autistic'. It was also almost a year after his initial grommet consultation that he had his Autism assessment.

Nothing could have prepared me for the mix of emotions I was going to feel when I heard the assessor confirm Kavi's Autism diagnosis out loud. Although I already knew, it didn't soften the blow, somehow, I thought it would. Knots in my stomach. Swallowing was no longer a matter of course as my throat began to dry up and breathing was elevated. It was officially official. I think up until that point I hadn't really dealt with the idea of him being autistic. Not really. I had not allowed my mind to worry about the future, I was very much about getting things done and not thinking about my emotions. I don't remember much after the confirmation whilst in the assessment room. I zoned out and began to worry about the future, what would I do next? What would his life look like? Would he be okay? What did this really mean? I finally felt like I was allowed to have these thoughts after swaying back and forth so many times. I just nodded as the assessor continued speaking without really taking anything in. Those 5 minutes seemed to last forever, and I felt like I was in a blur where time stood still. Of course, Kavi snapped me out of it by tugging at my hand continuously, he's always in a hurry! He wanted to leave as soon as we had arrived. I managed to hold the tears back until we got into the car.

I cried on and off for the 1-hour journey home. Crying because I was terrified, then getting angry at myself for crying. I'd hungered for his diagnosis for so long. I felt like I wasn't allowed to be upset. I wasn't thinking straight, repetitive thoughts going around in my head. It was really overwhelming because I couldn't decide how I was meant to be feeling. I was glad that Kavi was oblivious to the tears and was just in a hurry to get back to his safe place – home. Me too.

I hugged him so tightly that night and reminded myself that he was still the same beautiful boy that had walked into that assessment room. My happy and content little boy, always appreciative of the little things in life. I always said that I felt like I had cheated motherhood with him, regardless of the sleepless nights and worries around his food aversions. Every single day he would wake up with a smile on his face, he's even taught mummy to be a morning person!

Social media has really helped me personally in my healing. When Kavi was 1 and a half, I started my own small business which boomed during lockdown. I would post regularly on stories and sometimes talk about Kavi. Through this time, I met some amazing mums who helped me on my journey. Mona from Just Awesome and Sue, A Sprinkle on the Spectrum. Both have autistic children and the more they shared about their journey, the more it helped me to understand Kavi. I don't think they know just how much of an impact they've had and what an inspiration they are to me, even now.

Since January of this year, I've started to share Kavi and Nina's journey on TikTok. Talking and sharing helps me and I also know it's helping other parents along the way. Coming from a South Asian background, disabilities are not spoken about, and it's seen as a taboo subject. Many of my followers are from a South Asian background and I really hope I can help them and give them a safe space to talk too. It's so important to talk, there are people who can relate, and it helps everyone feel less alone.

There was a time period through lockdown where I came off my personal social media accounts because I would constantly be comparing Kavi to my friends' children, asking myself why he wasn't talking, why he wasn't doing all the things other children his age was doing. I was starting to resent my friends, as much as I was happy for them and their children it just cut too deep. I took a step back and I'm so glad I did. After a year I logged back in and found joy in seeing my friends' children thrive in their own way. I still have certain moments where my heart drops, I think we all do but I also always remind myself that I wouldn't change him for the world, he's perfect as he is and loved by so many including all of his 1-1's.

I remember going into the nursery to have a meeting with one of the owners and Kavi's 1-1. This was just after we suspected he had glue ear. They were really keen for me to get him an assessment because of the wait times, and I know it's because they already knew he was autistic but couldn't say it. My reply was 'I don't want to put a label on him if he doesn't need one'. This was my line of thinking, and it couldn't be any further from how I feel now, knowing it's a diagnosis and not a label. They were an amazing nursery and also a big part of our journey. Nina now attends the same nursery. I think they're proud of how far I've come because I am leading Nina's referral this time round. They've seen me grow as a person, and I have to say I'm really proud of myself too.

My daughter is 2 now and she's on the Autism pathway. If Nina had been my first child, I don't think I would have thought that she was autistic, but I know better now through experience of having Kavi and researching online. I spent that first year of her life watching and analysing her every move to see if I could see anything. I drove myself mad over it. I knew by 12 months that she was also autistic, I was expecting it, but I still think I'll be emotional the day of her diagnosis.

Kavi was 4 and a half when he got his diagnosis. It's hard for me to think back to how terrified I was on that day. I didn't think they were going to get better, my worries and fears about the future, but I was wrong. Sure, I have bad days/moments, but they are much less often, and I tend to recover from them a lot quicker and deal with my thoughts better. I'm still learning every-day.

The best piece of advice I've ever been given is take each day at a time. That really helps me because I'm a natural overthinker. I now also know to always trust my gut instinct when it comes to my kids. It's never been wrong.

My children reach milestones in their own time. Some milestones may seem so insignificant to a lot of parents, but they mean absolutely everything to me.

Watching the way they view the world is truly beautiful and pure, and it's not something every parent is lucky enough to experience.

I am so proud to be their mother, I will be their voice, I will always advocate for them, I will fight every fight for them, and I will always now trust my mother's instinct.

Sandeep Bains

About the Author

Sandeep Bains is a carer and mother of 2, currently fighting to get her Autistic son into a specialist school. She is also a stay-at-home mother to her 2-year-old daughter, who is on the Autism pathway. Sandeep recently closed down her successful small business, knitting chunky knit blankets, to focus on her children. She is passionate about advocating for her children, and offering support to other parents of neurodivergent children, by sharing relatable content on social media and sharing her journey as an SEN mother.

Chapter 12

Everything Finally Makes Sense

Kirsti Hadley

I n the summer of 2021, after travelling the long, exhausting journey to my child's autism, ADHD/OCD diagnosis, I too was diagnosed ADHD with autistic traits and dyscalculia. Suddenly, looking over my life through an alternate lens, everything finally made sense.

We spent from the age of 6 to 10, almost half of my child's young life at the time, fighting for their diagnosis. The admin and paperwork turned it into my full-time job, I had to completely re-learn and more importantly, unlearn ingrained neurotypical parenting strategies that were doing more harm than good without any support or assistance. I, like many others, had a very stereotypical image of what autism and ADHD looked like before I began my own research. Of course, that's why so many of us go undiagnosed for decades.

When the psychologist finally delivered Sonny's diagnosis, my child and I high-fived. When the same psychologist delivered my diagnosis he asked "how have you managed to stay alive this long?". We felt a huge sense of relief. Our efforts hadn't been in vain and our instincts had been right. These were celebratory and validating moments for us in contrast to the many lows we'd previously experienced following the advice from professionals, which was NOT to talk about ADHD or autism to them until we had a formal diagnosis.

One pivotal moment is ingrained in my memory. My child was in the bath one evening and they looked up at me and said completely out of the blue "mummy, I have seen so many doctors, why am I not fixed yet?" I looked at my child in disbelief, gobsmacked at how they had interpreted this process. How had I allowed this to happen? I decided there and then to take back control of our own narrative in a system that actively disempowers those of us with different brains. I explained to my child that there was nothing wrong with them, that there were two types of brain, neurotypical and neurodivergent, and that everyone needs to know which they have so that they can live, learn and work in a way that sees them thrive, not just about survive. Their answer, "oh, cool", proved to me that we do not need to dumb it down for our kids. It is far more damaging to tell a child that already knows they are different that they are wrong. If we withhold information and speak in hushed voices behind closed doors, children begin to catastrophise and jump to the worst possible conclusion. They think that they are faulty, broken, less than. When it comes to neurodiversity we are still living in the gap between the way things are and the way things should be. However, we have the power to use positive reinforcement in our own homes to counteract the negativity our children absorb, often at the hands of well-meaning people trusted to look after their best interests.

I start with the ending because I want to communicate in my chapter a term known as Familial Blindness. In a nutshell this means that, like me, many of us do not see how our children could possibly be autistic or ADHD because they are a chip off the old block. What we are now witnessing though, is a mass awakening of parents realising that not only are our kids ADHD/autistic, but we are too.

One of the biggest lessons this experience has taught me is the changes and support we're advocating for won't just help neurodivergent people; they will benefit everybody, and society overall. Learning, living and working in a neurodivergent way means everybody thrives. We are talking about human needs here, not special needs. Accessibility and inclusivity for all disabilities should be standard.

So, let's rewind. *Where did all of this begin?* My child hit all the traditional developmental milestones and, particularly as a toddler, was a bit of a wild child. But I was too, so we thought it was simply an inherited personality trait. My first suspicion that Sonny might be different came when one of their first school reports said they had a higher-than-normal grasp of the English language for a child of their age. They said Sonny was using that to avoid doing what teachers wanted them to. I present to you trait number 1; *demand avoidance.*

Then came trait number 2. So many *meltdowns* and *emotional dysregulation.* Again, because I had a similar disposition, we never thought to question it, but on closer inspection I noticed a pattern. The meltdowns would often come after a day at school masking.

Trait number 3. *Masking* is when autistic/ADHD kids learn to hide their traits for fear of being rejected or punished for them. Masking is exhausting and it often ends up in a big explosion of feelings when the child returns to their safe place, i.e. home, which is why it's so common for parents to hear the dreaded sentence "oh well they don't do that at school". Of course they don't, they are terrified of the repercussions.

Next, we have *intrusive thoughts*; trait number 4. Around this time, Sonny had developed what they named 'urges'. These presented as tapping their head repeatedly an equal number of times on the left side then the right. He also developed a fear of knives. We tried to find our own strategies to cope with it, like asking him to cut a tomato when we were making dinner. When we went for our private assessment, the Psychologist told me we'd developed our own form of cognitive behavioural therapy (CBT) for Sonny.

As parents, though, we'd just followed our instincts. They had just learned swear words at school. In fact, I remember them asking me if cud was the c word, to which I replied, 'yes babe, cud is definitely the C word!' Because my child knew that these words were taboo, the more they tried not to say them out loud the less they were able to hold them in, hence the urges pushed the swears out. Every other sentence became "fuck shit bitch cud". Raising a neurodivergent child is not the simplest of lives but one thing I can say without doubt is that it is never, ever boring. We can look back now and find the humour in this scenario but at the lowest moment, my child said that they couldn't cope anymore because their urges were taking over their entire life. But we got through it. One day about a month later the swearing just stopped. The swearing however was very distressing for my then 8 year old.

The turning point came when Sonny's trait number 5 appeared. This one could not be ignored because unlike the other traits, this was a physical and very visible trait, called *stimming*. Stimming is a self-stimulating behaviour that us autistics will do and while it can sometimes look like a tic, it's not; we use it to regulate. It can be something as small as wiggling our feet or playing with our hair. For me it's an eye stretch and a lot of blinking. For Sonny, it was hand flapping. The saddest thing was that early on they would hide to do it because they didn't think it was "normal". They do not hide this anymore. Once the stimming started, I fell down a google rabbit hole and became sure my child was autistic. That's when our journey to diagnosis really began in earnest. Sadly, my research confirmed that children's challenges are rarely taken seriously and oftentimes, parents aren't believed. The whole thing can be so unfair and inhumane.

After many meetings with the school, in which our concerns were dismissed as our child being 'quirky' and 'an enigma', we were eventually referred to our local authority for an assessment. Although we were lucky enough to have private healthcare insurance at the time, many providers don't cover private assessments for autism or ADHD. Although, ours did cover OCD which was part of the mix with Sonny. BRILLIANT, I thought, problem solved. Then another spanner in the works, Our local authority said they wouldn't accept a private assessment anyway, so we were effectively forced into joining this enormous waiting list and taking up a valuable space that could have been allocated to another child.

When we finally got the assessment date from our local authority, it was conducted over zoom (don't even get me started on the madness of this!) we anxiously awaited the results, only to be told that Sonny didn't present with the typical autistic symptoms. They could maintain eye contact, show empathy and make friends so they could not possibly be autistic.

Next, they informed us that Sonny would be referred for an ADHD assessment instead. This took us right back to square one, at the end of yet another years long waiting list. This time with CAMHS. It is wild to me that when our children are referred for one neurodivergent diagnosis they are not assessed for all at the same time. Dual-diagnosis is very common and this alters the presentation of traits, when the assessment came back as 'not autistic' it was heart-breaking and frustrating. They just couldn't see what was so obvious to us and worse, they would not believe us. I issued a complaint to our local authority and they agreed to reassess Sonny. But they'd already lost my trust and I knew we were going to be forced to prove them wrong, which didn't feel like a great start. Instead, I asked them to accept a private assessment and they agreed; something I wish had happened in the first place. It would have saved so much time and it would be a key piece of advice I'd give parents of autistic ADHD children. Don't just ask, stand your ground and insist. As the saying goes, it is better to ask for forgiveness than permission.

There's an interesting dichotomy when it comes to diagnosis. Often, in my experience, the authorities have historically only been interested in diagnosing us if we're causing a problem. I.e. disruptive at school or to society at large. However, when our struggles are more internal, then the powers that be turn a blind eye. It all comes down to how problematic we are. That said, more and more of us are now realising that while we as neurodivergent people might not be problematic for neurotypical society, neurotypical society can be very problematic for us. Definitely a contributing factor fuelling the surge in diagnosis. I myself had struggled internally my entire life as an undiagnosed woman and it all came to a head when I had one of those years where everything happens at once and it feels like your entire world is collapsing on top of you.

My mother died right before lockdown, my relationship with my child's dad broke down and I had Sonny at home during lockdown without a formal diagnosis. A best friend took her own life and I received a skin cancer diagnosis. Plus, I'd completely worked myself into the ground for decades. I had a breakdown. As I recovered I began therapy. It was only during one of those sessions that my therapist suggested I get my own assessment to see if I was ADHD autistic, too. I 100% believe that had I been diagnosed as a child I would have avoided that breakdown. Withholding diagnosis from our children now is a recipe for disaster down the line, and a potential mental health crisis far greater than the one we are currently in the midst of.

Sonny and I are still very much on a learning journey – together. Our conversations around neurodivergence are now very open and we follow a low-demand parenting strategy. It's been game-changing to find this new level of understanding with each other. We have slip ups, of course, but we are focused on improving our self-awareness and we're careful of how we broach certain subjects with each other. There's also a lot of what I call 'self-auditing', we pick things apart to understand how we can do better in the future. We have also learned to do a 'vibe check' in situations we find challenging. How do we feel before we do the thing, whilst we are doing the thing and again afterwards.

We have found this to be a very useful tool that allows us to work on further understanding how our neurodivergence shows up. There is a lot of common ground between neurodivergent humans, but we are each very unique too. It's important to recognise these differences so that we can be more accepting of one another and begin to set ourselves up for success, not failure.

So, where are we at now? We have our diagnosis, yay! Golden ticket! Problem solved. Well, not quite! Little did naive me realise that diagnosis was not the end but simply the beginning of the journey. Nothing really changes.

For a long time children struggling with school attendance have been incorrectly labelled 'school refusers' or 'ghost children', but a kinder term has now been coined; emotional based school avoidance, EBSA for short. Many of our children wake up to their morning alarm, eat breakfast and put their school uniforms on, only to find the idea of school so anxiety-inducing that it triggers panic attacks severe enough to prevent them even walking out of the front door. When you have seen this unfold in real life you know how cruel it feels to say that these children are refusing to go to school. They want to but they can't.

The first time I really listened to my gut around school was a long time after I should have. Again, following professional advice on how to be a good parent, I would persuade, distract, coerce and eventually force my child into school. The penny dropped on one particularly stressful drop-off, my child was at the school gates, red-faced hyperventilating, rigid, holding onto me for dear life and something in me just snapped. Why am I putting them through this? What could be the worst that would happen if they missed a day? So I said 'I am sorry but I am no longer forcing my child to do this'. I looked at Sonny and said 'come on, let's go home.' Their reply was heart-wrenching, 'THANK YOU FOR LISTENING TO ME MUMMY.' At the age of 9 my child had become so accustomed to having their needs ignored that they were grateful simply for being listened to - before they had even left Junior school.

Then we began the secondary chapter, yippee, 'it'll be a fresh start', they said. 'We can't start the EHCP process now', they said. 'We need a years' worth of evidence', they said. My child managed to attend secondary for just 3 months of year 7 before reaching burnout. It very nearly broke both of us. We are now navigating year 8 on a decreased timetable of 2-3 days per week, something we can all request and indeed insist upon for the sake of our family's mental health, but it is not common knowledge and it is local authority dependent. On the days my child is not in school, there is no alternate provision for their education, we are still stuck in this crazy, underfunded system.

6 years on from the beginning of our journey we do not have an EHCP in place. Even if we did there are no specialist school places available in our area. My child still calls school a kid prison and says it stands for Seven Cruel Hours of Our Lives. I no longer force my child to go to school, I allow them the space and grace to decide for themself. It is not easy. This approach comes with its own set of challenges. Particularly as a single parent. There have been periods of time where both my own and my child's mental health have suffered as a direct result of the pressure we are under, when I have been unable to work full time if at all. We have struggled to make ends meet financially, but slowly, one day at a time, sometimes even one hour at a time we are finding our groove as a duo. We have survived days that felt like they would never end, we have laughed until we couldn't catch our breath, and we even saw our first shooting stars together this summer.

The world, with its confusing neurotypical systems, standards, and people, continues to be tricky to navigate, but we are learning side by side. We have fought and continue to fight never-ending battles that only the other neurodivergent families around us can fully understand. We have got this far in spite of the people and systems that are supposed to help us, not because of them. I don't know what the immediate future holds for myself and my child, but I know we will be OK. I am SO proud of us and I am so proud of you, too.

Kirsti Hadley
About the Author

Kirsti Nicole Hadley, mum to Sonny-Jay, is a campaigner with SEND reform England and an inclusion consultant with @generationalaplhabet. After the confirmation of their own neurodivergence, and driven by a desire to avoid others experiencing the isolation and burnout they have, Kirsti and Sonny-Jay want to reframe the narrative around neurodivergence by promoting a mental health first dopamine driven approach to life.

From being expelled from school at 15, to being voted one of the most influential neurodivergent women of 2023, Kirsti is showing us that the future is neurodiverse!

Chapter 13

Bumpy Roads Often Lead To Beautiful Destinations

Rachel Wright

"**B**uckle up, mom. This is going to be a long journey!"

The words cut through me like a knife and pierced straight through my heart. With a huge lump in my throat and blinking away my watering eyes, I thanked the Speech and Language Therapist, left the Child Development Centre, walked back to my car, strapped Florence into her seat, climbed in and sobbed uncontrollably into the steering wheel.

Those words will be forever imprinted in my memory. It was the first time that a medical professional had ever said something that had shook me to my core and made me think long term. I had somehow convinced myself that Florence's speech loss was only temporary, and these words totally flipped that perception on its head. That morning, I walked into my first SALT appointment full of hope, like somehow the therapist would wave her magic wand and I would leave armed with a whole toolkit of strategies to unlock Florence's speech.

The reality however, was quite different. The therapist watched me intently and how I engaged with my little girl. Although she was lovely, I could not help but feel like I was being put to the test and judged. Was I doing something wrong? Had I not been interacting with her in the right way? After being told, I was 'doing all that I could' and given the reassurance I was using the correct strategies already, I could not help but feel totally deflated. The therapist must have sensed my desperation when I asked, "will she ever talk again?" It was in that moment she looked at me sympathetically, touched my arm and told me to, "buckle up!" I was so used to living in the here and now, trying desperately to pull Florence back into my world that I had never really considered what her future would look like.

You see, Florence used to talk. In fact, she did a lot of things before her regression. Over the period of just a few days, at 17 months, Florence lost all of her speech and the ability to clap, wave, use a spoon and drink from a cup. For a child who was usually so vibrant, engaging and smiley, it was almost as if somebody had turned out her light. She became insular and stopped engaging with me altogether – unless it was to open a food packet or help her get something she wanted. I was merely a tool to enable her to access the world. She had no interest at all in trying to engage with me for enjoyment or to seek comfort. I had no idea what was happening to my little girl and why she was behaving in this way. This period of confusion sent me into a spiral. Perhaps she was feeling under the weather? Or could it be because she was not attending nursery due to Covid-19 restrictions? For quite some time I buried my head in the sand and adopted a 'wait and see' approach. This proved to be unsuccessful. My usual methods of peekaboo and singing nursery rhymes did not appeal to her anymore and I had to relearn how to connect with my daughter all over again. Out of all the phases of Florence's development along her journey, the regression phase was most definitely the hardest.

Looking back, I did have an inkling when Florence was about 6 months that she may be Autistic. Although, it would not be until she was nearly 5 before we received her official ASD and GDD diagnosis. All day every day, her feet would constantly be rubbing together or rotating in circular motions. I only mentioned this to a few very close family members, due to fear of being ridiculed for thinking this of such a little baby. How could I possibly think she was Autistic this young? As family do, they reassured me and told me, "It is a sign of intelligence!" or "don't worry, she's perfect!" But something deep inside me, perhaps my mother's intuition, knew that Florence was not progressing at the same rate as her peers. In terms of developmental milestones, Florence seemed to be meeting them on time; she rolled at 6 months, crawled at 10 months and walked at 12 months. She babbled constantly and developed a vocabulary of about 20 words.

One thing I did notice early on were her lack of gestures. Florence never used her finger to point to anything and rarely waved goodbye. Something was niggling away at the back of my mind and I knew deep down that something was not quite 'right.' On toddler play dates, meeting up with my friends and their children, I started noticing gaps widen and her traits become more prominent. The differences were somehow more visible and I started comparing Florence more and more to her peers. I vividly remember going to visit a friend from work, whose son was just one month younger than Florence, and I ended up leaving their house in tears. Spending a significant chunk of time together, having a direct comparison side by side, I scrutinised every detail. My friend's son was bringing books and toys to share with his mother and their interactions were focused and reciprocal. Whilst Henry played with cars and took part in role play activities, Florence spent most of her time pacing back and forth in very repetitive motions and playing with the gravel under her feet. 'Perhaps it is because we have not been to their house before', I wondered. But the more I looked, the more I compared, the more my heart sank. What was happening to her? Why had she suddenly lost all these skills that she had previously mastered?

One evening, after sharing my concerns with Florence's father, I started Googling terms like, 'speech loss in toddlers.' I ended up falling down the rabbit hole of clicking on link after link spending hours trawling the internet in search of hope, in search of an answer. A common search result kept making an appearance; Autism. One particular site caught my attention about early signs of Autism in toddlers and as I read each bullet point the realisation began to sink in. Florence was Autistic! It was all there in black and white. Trait after trait. Sign after sign. Near enough, Florence was displaying nearly every single one! How had I not realised sooner? You see, nobody tells you about the early signs of Autism and what to look for in your children. Had I been more 'clued up' from the beginning, would I have spotted these signs at an earlier age? Would early intervention have made a difference?

When Florence first learnt to walk, she often crept up on her tiptoes. At first, I thought it was because she did not like going from one surface of flooring to another. Perhaps the laminate flooring was too cold? Now I know she was seeking sensory stimulation from the deep pressure under her foot. She did not follow my finger if I pointed to something or look behind her if I pretended to be excited or scared by something over her shoulder. Florence stopped responding to her name. She started to stack things and hold blocks in a very ordered and specific way with her fingers. Certain objects were only allowed on the lounge rug and she became obsessed with stretching and stacking her hair bobbles. She flapped her arms, held her fingers in tense postures, spun in circles and rocked back and forth. The signs were all there and it took me until 21 months to join the dots together and pluck up the courage to seek further support from our Health Visitor.

When I expressed my concerns to friends and family, some were quite dismissive. I do not think they had any intention of hurting my feelings, quite the opposite. It was almost as if they were trying to protect me and reassure me that all children do these things. I had so many tell me, "She's too young!"

"All children do that!" "she'll catch up." "She doesn't look Autistic." "Leave the poor kid alone – she's not even two yet!" With each dismissal of my concerns, I became less willing to share them with others. Unless people have experienced this journey for themselves, I don't think they will ever understand how isolating it can be and as time went on, I pulled myself away from others and began researching as much as I could to enable me to enter Florence's world.

Luckily, my Health Visitor did not dismiss my concerns and listened intently as I listed my pages of notes that I had made, linking them to the different areas of difficulty: social interaction, social communication, and restrictive or repetitive behaviours. She brought forwards Florence's 2-year developmental check and conducted a series of surveys, which showed Florence was significantly behind in certain aspects of her development. From her findings, she then made a referral to the Paediatrician and Speech and Language. 'That's it!' I thought. 'She is in the system, known to the services and NOW the real support will begin.' How little did I know...

We eagerly awaited our first paediatric appointment and luckily only had to wait for a few short months. Due to Covid-19, this was a telephone consultation. I was told it would be a long appointment and was excited to see what advice would be given out. Throughout the consultation, I went into great detail about my pregnancy and birth, tracing all aspects of Florence's development up until present day. The Paediatrician signposted me to a few websites and encouraged me to join an online 'course' for parents. It all felt very clinical and there was actually no advice given out at all, just a lot of questions about her diet, sleep habits, personal care, development, and autistic traits. Feeling frustrated with the system, I started looking elsewhere for support.

One Sunday morning, I plucked up the courage to take Florence to a SEND session at my local soft play centre. Walking in, my palms started to sweat, and I worried that people would think I was being 'silly' for taking my toddler to a session that was designed for children with additional needs and disabilities. I nervously scanned the room and made a few awkward smiles at other parents whilst I removed Florence's shoes.

Little did I know that 3 years later, this soft play session would form a huge part of my weekend routine and provide the best advice, support and friendship. These parents have lived experiences and many of them are much further down the line with their children's journey. Their words of wisdom are far more relatable than those printed within a leaflet or a website and I will be forever grateful for how the group welcomed me and took me under their wing. Not only is it a place where I can seek advice, but it is also a place where I can be myself – completely myself. I can parent Florence in the way that I need to, without the fear of being judged or being stared at by parents who do not quite understand. It is also a safe haven for Florence, where she can climb up the slide and slide down the steps, help herself to ice-lollies from the freezer without worried glances from the staff and she can stim away until her little heart is content. If you find something in your local area like this, grab it with both hands.

Parenting can be tough. Parenting children with additional needs can be even more so! The additional pressure of paperwork, appointments, online workshops, questionnaires, application forms, EHCP deadlines, meetings, emails, and telephone calls can take its toll on any relationship. Statistically, the percentage of parents who separate whilst raising disabled children is significantly higher than parents of neurotypical children. I never thought I would ever become part of that statistic and find myself as a single parent. Yet, back in January 2023, that is precisely the situation I found myself in. At first, I wondered how I would cope and how Florence would adapt to our new living situation with co-parenting. However, months down the line, we have navigated our new path together, mother and daughter, finding our new rhythm and dancing to our own beat.

Our journey has not always been easy, but our incredible bond makes every day worthwhile. Who knows what our future may hold and what challenges we are yet to face? All I know is that, as long as I am on this earth, I will be right by Florence's side to face those things together. Mother and daughter against the world. They say that Autism does not come with an instruction manual but comes with a parent who will never give up. I will never stop fighting for her and advocating for others to give them the best possible chance in life. She has changed me in ways that I never thought possible. She has shown me how to be a more empathetic, patient and a considerate person, and moulded me exactly into the parent that I needed to be.

I will be forever grateful to her for teaching me these things and feel so proud that I was chosen to be her mum.

Rachel Wight

About the Author

Rachel Wright is one of the founding members of SEND Reform England and recognises that 'Difficult Journeys often lead to beautiful destinations.' She is a teacher and leader in a mainstream school, with a keen passion for SEND provision. Having seen EHCPs in action in mainstream classrooms, she knows how crucial they are to ensure children's well-being and success.

Rachel is a proud single mother, raising an Autistic and globally delayed daughter. She is enthusiastic about sharing her experiences with others, ensuring they don't feel alone whilst navigating their own journeys. Feeling incredibly grateful to be part of an amazing community of SEND parents, she has relished the opportunities that SEND Reform has offered.

Chapter 14

Tourette's and Us

Jodie Lynn

I guess the only place to start is at the beginning and I'll share my thoughts and feelings along the way.

Tourette's syndrome is a condition of the nervous system. It causes people to have something called "Tics'. Tics are sudden movements, twitches, or sounds. People who have tics are not able to stop their body from doing these things.

My daughter Nicole is unfortunately one of the 300,000 children/adults living with this debilitating disability in the UK.

Tourette's is an inherited neurological condition and seeing as how I'm super broken it stands to reason that my children will inherit quirky traits from me. Before anyone reading this thinks 'how she can be so disrespectful to firstly her daughter, and secondly to a person with a disability?' Think for a second about the challenges parents like myself face on a daily basis, and how any human could possibly cope and overcome all the overwhelming feelings that come from having children who are disabled. Humour is our go to for everything, because as I'm sure you hear from most parents such as myself, if you didn't laugh you would cry.

I'm a huge advocate for children with disabilities. My son was diagnosed at 4 years old with a severe delay in speech, language and communication. I was raised by parents who did respite care for young disabled adults. We spent many summers with different young people, making so many wonderful memories of hanging on to the edge of wheelchairs. Paul, who used to come regularly, let me steer his electric wheelchair. Needless to say, I wasn't allowed to do it much as we went over a speed bump and almost tipped us both out. I feel like I was a lucky child having the experiences I had and learning to respect and love so many different people from a young age. I truly believe things happen for a reason and me becoming the mum I am for my three quirky kids was just fitting.

I often joke about the meme saying 'God gives the biggest battles to the strongest warriors' because I didn't ask to be a warrior, nor did my children. I mean, I don't even believe in God let's not get into that debate though, save that for another time. But what I do believe is that I'm the right person to fight for my children. I'm the mum who shouts the loudest to enable them to have all the same chances as any other person.

Nicole copes so incredibly well having this disability, she is so strong and brave. I'm not even sure I would cope as well as she does on a daily basis. Don't get me wrong, on days when it's at its worst, Nicole has something called 'tic attacks.' This simply means the tics are non-stop and usually violent; she can injure herself and others around her. They are painful and can last anywhere between 30 mins and 7 hrs, that's been her longest attack. During these periods, it's a constant assessment of where we are, how we can keep her and others safe, and timing to see if it's to a point where we need to seek medical intervention from emergency services. I reckon I'm a dab hand at risk assessments and could definitely earn an absolute mint doing that job for someone as I literally do it on the daily! Plan A. Plan B, usually A and B go Pete Tong and we end on Plan T, that I make up on the spot!

Nicole has been hospitalised on numerous times over the years due to her Tourette's. These attacks then wipe Nicole out mentally and physically for the next few days. The constant body movements are physically exhausting for her. Not to mention the effect it has on the rest of the family. Her two young brothers have had to learn how to cope with not only Nicole's feelings, but their own when she tics. Nicole's tics can be funny, scary, rude and even hurtful at times; saying things she is most definitely not thinking or feeling, but tics it, nonetheless. The boys have had to learn that it's not what their sister is, which enables them to accept that she can't help it. Freddie is my youngest son, and he was just 7 /8 years old when she first started to tic, so it was a lot to comprehend for such a young man. Freddie is now one of Nicole's biggest supporters. When we are out and about, and he sees people stare or say things, he's straight in there protecting her and standing up for her. Jayden, although non-verbal when he was younger, (we have our own story regarding his personal journey) is able to speak now. Although he doesn't see things the same as everyone else, he has also learnt how to support and understand his big sister. He also has a lot of courage and strength, supporting her when she is having a bad tic day.

I must just share one funny story showing the difficulties Jayden struggles with. Jayden has undiagnosed Asperger's. We had lots of assessments when he was younger and I wished I had pushed for a label, but at the time I didn't want that to hold him back in his future, nor did I want to label him something that could be used negatively against him. Due to the fact we had an EHCP in place from the age of 4, and he had a one-to-one support worker for the maximum hours, it wasn't worth pushing because he had what he needed to complete his day-to-day school life. Anyway, that was some background to better understand the story, which I'm now writing and probably won't be as funny as I thought at the time.

Nicole was having a bad tic day that soon escalated into a tic attack. We were at home and Nicole and I were downstairs. Freddie came in and asked if we needed more pillows or a glass of water (that's his go to, to feel useful, bless him).

Anyway, I will set the scene. I am physically holding Nicole's arms on the floor by the sofa to stop her thumping herself in the face and punching the floor. Nicole's crying and asking me to make it stop which is just the worst as a parent. Jayden pops his head round the door, 'mum can I have a bag of crisps?' Me, 'can you just give me a min Jay I'm sorting Nicole?' Jay, 'ok' ... Off he goes. Less than two minutes passes and he's back at the door. 'So, mum, can I have the crisps?'. I kid you not this kid is completely oblivious to the situation unfolding in front of him and is solely focused on a bag of crisps. And in that moment, I literally laughed out loud and said, 'yeah just go grab them.' Even Nicole, in the state she was in, looked at me like 'typical Jay.' Like I said, if you didn't laugh, you would cry.

Tourette's is often mistaken for just swearing randomly at people. This is only part of it, and the people who actually do have the swearing tics only make up 10% of those who have Tourette's. I think the reason people associate this as being Tourette's is due to the media coverage of the disability over the years. I completely agree that people with Tourette's are absolutely hilarious, and Nicole should definitely be on the TV because she is just a whole vibe. Tics or not, she has this aura that sets her apart from others. We like to share the funny moments and raise awareness of this disability as, like I said, most people assume it's just swearing. There is so much more to it than that. The way it affects the whole family, not just the person with the disability. I think that goes for most households who have a child or adult with a disability; it's something that everyone has to learn ways to navigate through. I really hope reading this small chapter from me has opened your eyes to see things differently and support more people who are struggling for whatever reason. Ultimately, children are our future and, as adults we have a responsibility to show our children to treat others how you want to be treated. Respect costs nothing and understanding is something you choose to have.

Our story is continuing, as are many others. If you are in a position to help, share, etc then honestly it costs nothing to do so. Right now, so many parents are fighting for their children's basic rights for EHCPs. My son was lucky enough to get his at a young age due to his conditions. He has continued to do well at school simply because this was in place. Although he has his, and I don't need to fight for it, I'm still standing by all the people who weren't as lucky as my son; all those children who need the same educational support that my son is getting.

I will leave my chapter by saying simply this; 'becoming a parent brings so many emotions you never knew existed, becoming a parent of a child with disabilities brings a strength you never knew you had.'

Jodie Lynn

About the Author

Jodie Lynn is a gym loving mum of 3 soon to be married and become Jodie Dyer. Jodie is the founder of a successful registered charity, Jodie's Cyprus Dogs Rehoming. She is also a content creator, raising much needed awareness for Tourette's syndrome and educating people on all aspects of the disability.

Jodie's daughter, Nicole, started to tic at age 13 and was later diagnosed with Tourette's. Jodie describes herself as having a 'zest for life and a dark, inappropriate sense of humour!'

Chapter 15

Tales With A Twist

Charlie Beswick

'Your son has been born with half a face'.

Okay, so that's not exactly what the consultant said, but it's basically what it boiled down to.

I had undergone an emergency caesarean a couple of hours earlier and had delivered twin boys. I had assumed that they were healthy. Why wouldn't they be? I don't smoke, hadn't drunk alcohol, ate well and never, not once, did I think I'd have anything other than two perfectly formed, healthy children. But now I was being told otherwise.

Mark, my fiancé, was sitting to my left having just come back from making all the customary phone calls to announce the safe arrival of two boys. The midwife had popped her head into my cubicle while he had been gone and said that she'd come back when Mark was with me. I remember that her smile made me feel uneasy for a moment, but it passed as quickly as it came. I was still 'fuzzy' from the drugs and very tired, and so I dismissed my brief concern.

Once Mark was with me, the consultant came and sat at the foot of the bed, and Sarah, a lovely midwife about the same age as me, sat next to him, to my right. I remember being aware that she was watching me intently. Now I know why.

The consultant, Dr Mona, explained that twin one (Oliver) was fine, but twin two (Harry) had some problems. I can still see the way that Dr Mona drew an imaginary line down the centre of his face with his hand and swept it across to the left side as if he were erasing what was there. I processed it all in painfully slow motion, as if I were dreaming. His voice was muffled as if he was talking to me underwater. I could hear the odd word, dulled by my delayed understanding and the pounding in my ears. At the same time, he was mentioning something about no eye, a small, under-developed ear, no nostril, a short and slanted jaw. He mentioned Golden something syndrome and Hemi something or other. I now know these to be Goldenhar syndrome and Hemifacial Microsomia – different terms for similar conditions. Associated with this condition are heart defects, spinal problems and brain damage, but it was too early to know how severely Harry had been affected. He'd also been born with only one artery in his umbilical cord instead of two and the implications of this were, again, unknown at that time.

Dream. Bad dream. Thick, thick fog. What?

I remember looking from Dr Mona to Mark repeatedly as he told us the news like a person would look to a translator for help understanding a foreign language. I couldn't process this information. Not us. Not me. No. I felt as though I was drowning. This wasn't what was supposed to happen. Parents were told the weight of their babies. That it was time to hold and cuddle them. They would gaze into their little eyes and pour themselves into their perfect creation feeling an elation beyond anything they had ever known. It must be a mistake.

I sat perfectly still, frozen in that moment that I would relive for years to come. All I could whisper as fat, slow tears rolled down my face was, 'I'm sorry. I'm sorry'. No hysterical outbursts or sobbing convulsions. Just a paralysis of disbelief and guilt.

Despite being shocked and stunned, I found the guilt overwhelming. Mark squeezed my hand and told me I had nothing to be sorry for. Dr Mona also assured me that it wasn't due to anything that I had or hadn't done throughout the pregnancy, but I couldn't think of anything else. When did it all go wrong?

Think, Charlene. Think. What did you do? What have you done to your child?

Hot on the tail of guilt came a much darker emotion. Fear. Dr Mona sat in front of me, describing a baby who only had half a face and, for all we knew, no quality of life ahead of him, and yet I was expected to love him. But what if I couldn't? What if I couldn't look at him, let alone hold him or bond with him? What if I was repulsed by this strange looking baby that I'd not expected or prepared for? Surely everyone would know just by looking at me, I wasn't the mother this boy needed.

When Sarah asked if I wanted to see him, I was absolutely terrified. Seeing him was the last thing that I wanted to do at that moment, but I said yes. What else could I say? What sort of cold, hard, unfeeling, wicked (feel free to add your own adjectives) person would I have been to admit my fears to anyone? It's only now when I reflect on those moments that I realise they were perfectly normal.

By now I had called the one person who I felt had the magical power to make this all right for me, to hold me through my nightmare and shush it all away. I don't remember what I said to my mum on my phone in the hospital bed. I know that I whispered, partly because only a thin curtain separated us from a ward full of mothers I no longer had anything in common with, partly because

I knew that the alternative to whispering would drain me of any bit of energy I now had left. I think I said, 'Something is wrong', and I cried. Mum left work immediately to come to us.

Many years later, when I faced all these feelings in the safe space of a therapeutic setting, I pictured a vase. Beautiful, big and colourful, but it had been smashed into hundreds of pieces. Every fragment had been retrieved and painstakingly reassembled so to all the world it still looked like the proud vase it once was. It still did the same job, but it was a fragile version of its former self. Changed forever. That moment, that day, was when my vase tipped off the edge of its table, hit the floor and shattered.

I don't know how long it was before the wheelchair came to take me to the Special Care Baby Unit (SCBU). The excitement that had filled me less than 24 hours ago felt like someone else's now, and all I had left was fear, dread and a sickness in the pit of my stomach. I forced a smile and got in the wheelchair. It was time to meet my boys.

Over the next six years, I battled massively with my mental health but hid it behind a smile that I now call 'the lie we wear'. Everyone had told me that I could do this, that I was the best mum for my boys. As much as it was amazing to have their belief, it set a really high bar for me to live up to. I still felt like such a failure so I kept my feelings to myself rather than disappointing people.

When I look back at Harry's baby photographs now, I see the most gorgeous twinkly eye and cheeky smile but back then, all I could see was my inability to give him even a face. I felt like the worst mother in the world, but I loved my boy very much. When Harry was 3 and a half he was diagnosed as autistic and, a year later, Mark and I divorced after only being married for 3 years.

As a single parent, I was juggling Harry's reconstruction operations, therapies and appointments and the demands of my teaching career on the very little sleep that many autistic children allow us. When the before and after school provision that cared for my boys informed me that they couldn't help me anymore, I had to leave teaching.

We lose so much don't we - our careers, our identity, our friends sometimes, our self-confidence, our dreams. It's a grief that I poured onto paper and then published 'Our Altered Life' in 2017. It was amazing to hear from other mums who truly understood me in ways that my own family and friends simply couldn't and who, in turn, felt seen by reading my words. It's one of the reasons why I was keen to be included here. We feel more alone than we really are at times.

For me, I see now that I created the isolation myself. I was adamant that I wasn't going to be 'one of those' special needs mums at the beginning. My boys would be fine. I could cope alone. I believed that I could get everything I needed from the remnants of the life I had planned.

It was a dream that I had to let go of and it was so very painful at times.

I am reminded daily by strangers' looks, stares, and whispers that my son looks different. I often deal with online trolls telling me my son shouldn't be alive. I battle constantly for him to have access to the things that so many others take for granted. My soul feels bruised at times, tender and raw but my boys are worth it all.

In the beginning, people would say 'special children only get sent to special parents' and I wanted to scream at them. Their hearts were in the right place, but they were so very wrong. Children like Harry are sent to ordinary parents all the time. Some decide that the special needs life just isn't for them, and they decide to have their child adopted. Some neglect their children and themselves because the reality and emotions that come with a life like ours are just too big for them. Then there are the parents who are incredibly ordinary but whose children transform them into strong, brave, persistent advocates who worry daily that they are failing their children, when in fact they are safer, better fed and more loved than so many others. Why are we so hard on ourselves in ways that we would never be to a friend?

I have learned so much as the mum of my boys and I have to give a shout-out to Oliver. Siblings are the unsung heroes of our stories, and he is the most incredible young man not despite his life but because of it all. It's not a life I would have chosen for him, but I am so very proud of him.

Nowadays, I have remarried, and we have the most incredible blended family who see each other as siblings. I am still making a difference as I strived to do as a teacher but just in different ways. I founded a charity called More Than a Face to educate children and young people on visible differences. I want to encourage them to see people for who they are, not just what they look like. The journey of Our Altered Life continues on social media with a community that truly treasures my boys. I also mentor mums just like me and you in my SEND Gin and Cheese community (because I would have never joined SEND help and support).

Over eighteen years after having my life turned upside down and inside out in the swipe of Dr Mona's hand, I have learnt that it's all a process and nothing lasts forever; sometimes not even the progress (regression is so hard) and mainly not the challenges. They sure as hell don't disappear but they do change.

We change.

I know now that it's important we don't believe what we think about ourselves all of the time, that it's essential we have our pity parties but equally vital that we don't unpack and live there. We need to forgive ourselves for the things that were never actually our fault in the first place. In taking one day at a time, the future takes care of itself. Even tales with a twist can have a happy ending.

Charlie Beswick

About the Author

Charlie Beswick is mum to 18-year-old twins, Oliver and Harry. She is the author of the best-selling book Our Altered Life, a brutally honest account of how she came to terms with a life she never expected. She is also an award-winning blogger and her family's story has been featured internationally on Sky Tv and national press.

Charlie founded SEND Gin & Cheese CIC to support maternal mental well-being at the point of their child's diagnosis and beyond. She also founded More Than a Face charity and has spoken with over 7000 students to educate them on visible differences, including behaviours typically associated with autism. She is a teacher with over 16 years of experience in both primary and secondary schools.

Chapter 16

The Only Fucks To Give – As A SEN Mother

Hannah Gibbard

R aising a child with both Attention Deficit Hyperactivity Disorder (ADHD) and Autism Spectrum Condition (ASC), comes with its own set of daily challenges, and I'm not talking about your child's challenges!

Like many mothers of children with special educational needs (SEN), I have experienced intense worry to the point of despair, extreme loneliness, overwhelm from the constant battles (from getting a diagnosis to securing the right school) and exhaustion levels that rival those you only *normally* endure when you have a newborn baby. My son is now 11 and he still struggles with sleep... When I say 'he', I mean 'we'! We struggle with sleep. On the rare occasion that I accidentally 'nod off' before him, I can guarantee he will be awake (gaming, watching or scrolling) ALL night.

As my son was my first child, I was unsure initially whether some of the behaviours he displayed by the time he reached his toddler years, e.g.

endless energy, difficulty sleeping, chronic anxiety, emotional dysregulation and frequent meltdowns, were typical for a 'spirited but sometimes shy/sensitive' young boy, or whether something more complex was going on below the surface.

It was at his first parent teacher meeting, six weeks after he started Reception year of primary school, that the word 'Autism' was mentioned. I remember feeling angry that it had taken the teacher six weeks to say anything, but not altogether surprised by her observations. Back then, little did I know that delays would be a frequent feature of our future. Fast forward 20 months, when he received his formal diagnosis of Autism Spectrum Condition, the predominant emotion, upon hearing those words, was that of relief. Deep down, I had known for a long time and my concerns which had previously been batted away by friends and even professionals, were validated. Was I worried about what his future would hold? Yes. But at least I knew what we were dealing with.

The feedback from the initial ASC diagnosis, included a referral for an ADHD assessment. He was diagnosed with ADHD combined type (impulsive, inattentive, and hyperactive) the following year, at 7 years old. I recall a couple of things from the ADHD diagnosis appointment. Firstly, he bounced a ball against the wall of the clinic repeatedly, despite being asked to stop. He made the assessing doctor's job pretty easy! Secondly, when he asked what we were doing there, I explained ADHD and said, 'maybe that sounds like you', to which he responded, 'Obviously. I could have told you that! Can we go now?' He's a sharp cookie, with a tendency to voice his opinion (generally, black and white, no grey area) but he'd rather not look you in the eyes whilst delivering his often accurate thoughts, and you'd probably have to meet him a few times before he'll speak to you at all. He once asked, quite innocently, 'what is *normal* about staring at someone's eyeballs anyway?' He's got a point.

Explaining ADHD and ASD to my son at a young age happened quite naturally, in a conversational way, as a result of his brilliant, enquiring mind.

I'm grateful for that as I know some parents struggle with deciding when to talk to their child about their diagnoses. My son's reaction to the news of his diagnoses was refreshingly matter-of-fact and it quickly became evident that he saw these conditions as part of his identity, rather than something to be stigmatised or hidden. He's emerged as a staunch advocate for the perspective that these neurodivergent traits are not disabilities but rather different abilities, unique lenses through which he views the world.

My main challenge now is helping him to develop tools to assist with his impulsiveness. His go-to response when he answers back *over and over again* tends to be, 'can't help it. ADHD.' Yes, being his parent is a work in progress, the steepest of learning curves. I'm 11 years into this SEN motherhood journey and I still haven't got a clue what I'm doing! They say babies don't come with a manual. Well, if they DID come with a manual, my baby would have ripped it up and set it on fire... metaphorically, obviously. There's no rule book here, and very few rules in our house at all, if I'm being totally honest. I never thought I'd be that Mum who would allow electronics at the dinner table. I say dinner table, but I actually mean whilst eating dinner on the sofa, or under the table or in his bedroom. Wherever the location, I can guarantee that electronics are involved. Others may judge and to my regret, what other people think used to affect me intensely. I remember the looks of horror whenever I talked about 'bedtime' in our house. Another ongoing battle. Gradually, and it's taken years, I have stopped caring, for the most part, what other people think. Here's the secret to help with that... the three little words that you <u>need</u> to hear if any of the above sounds vaguely familiar: FIND YOUR TRIBE.

One of the most profound aspects of raising a child with ADHD and ASD is the feeling of loneliness. It's not just the physical isolation, though that can be a part of it, especially when well-meaning friends and family members struggle to understand the daily challenges we face. It's also the emotional isolation, the feeling that no one truly comprehends what it's like to walk in our shoes. It's often hard to find fellow parents who can relate to the specific challenges we face. While I appreciate the support of close friends and family, many of whom have taken the time to become informed about Autism and ADHD, there's something uniquely comforting about connecting with other mothers who are navigating a similar path. Amid the struggles and loneliness, I discovered the invaluable lifeline that is my reliance on other SEN mothers. These women, who have children with a range of special educational needs, became my tribe, my confidants, and my source of strength. I know how incredibly lucky I am to be a part of SEND Reform England. Having a SEN mum support system on speed dial has been life changing. We speak daily and we laugh, we cry, and we provide each other with the understanding that only someone who's been through it can offer. I've learned practical strategies for managing daily life with a child with ADHD and ASD, but most importantly, I've found a safe space to express my fears and frustrations, knowing that I'm not alone on this journey.

The very best advice I can give to any parent of a SEN child, is do whatever you need to do to surround yourself with others who GET IT. Who don't judge. Who don't look or sound shocked when you explain that your child has refused to go to school for days/weeks on end. *'No Margaret, I can't just drag them there/ force them to go/ inflict and cement further trauma after years of feeling misunderstood in an institution solely designed for the neurotypical!'* Sorry, that's a different rant and I'll come to that shortly.

I'll end this part by once again, *insisting* that you find someone in the same (or similar) boat to whom you can offload. Whether they are local, or online, an existing friend or a new connection. Find them. Your own sanity depends on it.

When it comes to education, it deeply frustrates me to witness how neurodivergent children, like my son, are often expected to conform rigidly to the social standards and norms of the neurotypical world, particularly within the confines of the school environment. This expectation can be suffocating, forcing them into a mould that doesn't fit their unique neurology. Our schools should be places that celebrate these differences, providing tailored support and understanding rather than enforcing conformity. Witnessing my child grapple with issues of self-esteem, social difficulties, and an ever-present sense of feeling different is nothing short of heart-wrenching. It's a pain that ran deep, as I saw him navigate a world that often fails to fully appreciate his unique qualities. The moments when they doubt themselves or express feelings of isolation are like daggers to the heart, reminding me of the daily battles faced by him and others like him.

My role as a SEN solicitor has been a blessing in my journey as a mother to an Autistic child with ADHD. My job has given me the opportunity to speak with other SEN parents every week, offering them not only legal advice but also feelings of solidarity and the overriding message that they are not alone in their struggles. I've had the privilege of reassuring other parents that their thoughts are valid, and their concerns are heard. Many times, the parents I speak with are learning to cope with the same judgments and misunderstandings that I face daily. It's a comfort for them to know that I, too, have walked this path and can empathise with their experiences.

While the legal aspects of navigating the SEN system can be daunting, I help parents understand their rights and advocate for their child's needs within the legal framework. The battle to secure the right support in school for my own child, including the fight for an Education, Health, and Care Plan (EHCP), has been a lengthy, draining and emotionally overwhelming process. It's a journey that requires tireless advocacy, countless meetings, and an unwavering commitment to the pursuance of my child's legal right to a suitable education. The EHCP process, in particular, has tested my resilience as a parent, as it often involves navigating bureaucratic hurdles and protracted waiting times. Throughout this challenging process, I've learned that developing a relentless fighting spirit is essential. I would advise other parents to keep going, for they have no choice but to advocate for their child; if they do not, no one else will.

For many, the right support is not only what a child deserves, but what they NEED, in order to survive.

Anxiety, OCD, and the soul-destroying spectacle of self-harm is a painful journey no child, or their parent, should ever have to endure. I can only describe it as a crushing weight of helplessness that presses down as you witness the relentless turmoil within them. Anxiety tightens its grip around their mind, creating a constant state of unease and doubt. OCD whispers its irrational demands, forcing the child into compulsive rituals and endless loops of obsession. The most agonising of all is the self-harm, the physical manifestation of their inner turmoil, a cry for relief from the emotional pain. My heart aches with the knowledge that my son has to live with these heavy burdens. He is a CHILD.

Discovering the right school is now playing a huge part in helping him deal with these struggles, the hugely negative aspects of Autism, ADHD and associated issues. Finally, he is in an environment where hopefully, he can shed the weight of constant masking and be himself. He has only just started secondary school, a small independent school with a focus on SEN, after years of 'surviving not thriving' in a local, mainstream primary school. Whilst he may have appeared to be coping at his previous school, his frequent post-school meltdowns indicated otherwise.

The "Coke bottle effect" is a stark reality in the life of a child, like my own, battling ADHD and ASD. Throughout the school day, they clasp the lid on their emotions tightly, masking their struggles, conforming to societal expectations, and navigating the overwhelming sensory environment. It's a draining, herculean effort to maintain composure in a world that often misunderstands them. Then, the moment they step into the safety of their home, the pressure builds like carbonation in a shaken soda bottle. It's only a matter of time before the lid flies off, resulting in explosive meltdowns or emotional eruptions. While these moments were challenging for both my son and our family, they serve as a poignant reminder of the incredible effort it takes to navigate a neurotypical world as a neurodivergent individual.

Recently, he has come home from his new school tired but happy - actually smiling! This never happened before, and I get incredibly emotional thinking about that. I believe that specialist schools for SEN children offer several distinct advantages over mainstream schools, even for students, like my son, who can access the National Curriculum. One crucial advantage is the tailored and supportive environment that specialist schools provide. These schools are equipped with staff who are trained to *understand* the specific needs of neurodivergent students - teachers and support staff are experienced in working with SEN children and young people.

Teaching staff need more than half a day of INSET training to understand the complexities of the vast autism spectrum. Specialist schools typically have smaller class sizes, which is particularly beneficial for anxious pupils or those who may struggle in larger, more overwhelming mainstream classrooms. What I appreciate most about my son's new secondary school, is the fact they prioritise the well-being of their students. They create an environment that fosters emotional and social development, reducing stress and anxiety levels, which can be particularly high for neurodivergent children in mainstream settings. When he progresses into Year 8, for example, meditation and mindfulness are part of the curriculum. Practices that I hope will play a part in overcoming the demons of anxiety, OCD and self-harm that haunted his younger years. I'm also grateful that he is finally among peers who share similar challenges, which should reduce feelings of isolation and foster a sense of belonging. This is crucial for my son who, like many of us, neurodivergent or otherwise, holds a deep desire to form friendships and to be accepted, appreciated, and liked by those around him.

I once heard that SEN parents have similar stress levels to that of army combat soldiers. I can confirm that this is true... in my own personal experience anyway! I have been an SEN mother for over a decade now, but I still say, 'I'm here for legal advice, not parenting advice.' I confess that I am still clueless when it comes to many of the daily parenting struggles. What I will say to any fellow SEN mum, is that you need to trust your instincts when it comes to YOUR child and try your hardest to stop caring about the judgement of others, particularly when 'parent blame' is involved. That's my biggest pet hate. Mother to mother, these are the only Fucks you need to give (care about):

1. Finding your tribe - this is the no.1 piece of advice. Other SEN parents can be a lifeline and will help you through the darkest days, reminding you that you are not alone.

2. Fighting spirit - it shouldn't be a battle to get the right support for our children but sadly it often is. I speak to parents every week who are on this seemingly endless road to securing appropriate provision, setting and a suitable education for their SEN child. Keep going.

3. Facts - know your stuff when it comes to your child's conditions and needs. Read books, take courses, listen to podcasts and learn from other SEN parents. You need to try and understand what they are dealing with and see the world through their eyes. You also need to know what you are legally entitled to when it comes to support and schooling. Local authorities and SENCos are not always accurate in their advice so think about getting some decent legal advice to secure what your child is entitled to!

4. Failure is fine - becoming a SEN parent involves a MASSIVE learning curve. Put frankly, life and parenthood may not be what you expected them to be. You'll get things wrong, you'll have regrets, you'll wish you knew things sooner, but that's OK. None of us were born experts. Don't beat yourself up. There are weeks when I cry most days through the frustration and exhaustion of it all. But the reality is, I would never change my son and I'll never stop trying to learn how to be the best mother to him.

Josef is, without a doubt, the love of my life. Like all classic love stories, we go through incredible highs and unbelievable lows. Being his mother is the hardest job I've ever had. But also, the one job I will cherish for the rest of my days.

Hannah Gibbard

About the Author

Hannah Gibbard is a SEN lawyer who advocates for parents to secure the right education and support for their children. Her background in criminal defence means she is adept at dealing with those who, on occasion, turn a blind eye to the law. This has been particularly useful when dealing with certain Local Authorities!

Hannah has two children, one of whom is an Autistic ADHDer. She is a coffee addict whose limited spare time is spent catching up with the fabulous women of SEND Reform England and living vicariously through the Real Housewives of Everywhere.

Chapter 17

Together, we always find a way; our way

El Jedras

I never really thought I'd be a mum. To be honest, I never saw kids on my future path. But life has a funny way of surprising us, doesn't it? Now, I'm a mum to three amazing children. I call them my little heroes. I can't imagine my world without them.

My journey into motherhood took an unexpected route. Medical issues early in life had doctors telling me that having kids might not be in the cards for me. And then there was that one defining moment—a memory etched deep into my soul. I was just 17, still figuring out life, when I found myself in the midst of childbirth. It was my close relative, and it happened right at home. I was the only one there to help, and it was far from the serene, beautiful birth we see in movies. It was tough, raw, and life-changing and a loss I am still healing from today. I saw the pain, the struggle, and the unpredictability of it all. It was a lot to handle for a young teenager. That experience left a lasting impression on me and a deep sense of responsibility. After this defining moment I felt confident that a child was the most beautiful gift to be given, but this just wasn't for me.

So, becoming a mother was a journey I hadn't planned for, but it was one I was ready to embrace when the time came, and I met my soul mate. It was almost a deal breaker for us to be together, but somehow, as I saw my 30th birthday approaching, I had matured into the notion that a child would be a truly beautiful gift. I already knew this might be a challenge, and it definitely wasn't as simple as we had hoped both physically and mentally. After three heart-breaking miscarriages, we finally welcomed our firstborn, Ruby, into the world.

Ruby was magnificent. I was in love the moment I met her. She was the most amazing little thing, and I remember spending days and days just holding her, tears in my eyes, wondering why I ever doubted the idea of being a mother. The love I felt for her was something so unique and special that I knew this is where I was always meant to be, and fear was no longer going to hold me back from being a mum.

Little did I know that this path would lead me to a new world of motherhood, a world I had never imagined; the world of Special Educational Needs and Disabilities (SEND).

My first born, Ruby, continued to amaze me at every stage. Everyone who met her would gush about how incredible she was. I actually grew used to people saying she "blew them away," and I eagerly looked forward to their compliments. I was one very proud mommy. She was exceptionally bright and sailed through all her milestones. I cherished her little quirks, like the way she meticulously separated all the colours of her Legos and toys. I loved watching her expertly stack things over and over again, or arrange her crayons, toys, and even her food in precise lines. Those quirks were what made her uniquely herself.

But then, the notorious "terrible two's" hit us like a ton of bricks, and it hit hard. I remember saying, just days after her 2nd birthday, that she had changed almost overnight. Ruby seemed to grow easily frustrated, and meltdowns became a regular occurrence, seemingly out of nowhere. They were so difficult and painful to watch. Nothing I did could calm her; she would become wild with anger, and each episode seemed to break me piece by piece, day by day.

I tried all the things I had been taught— different calming techniques, time outs, taking away toys, ignoring her tantrums—but none of them seemed to work. If anything, these approaches made things worse. One day, I reached my breaking point. I screamed at her, telling her to stop and that I had had enough. I just wanted my happy little girl back. She was momentarily shocked by the intensity of my voice but quickly spiralled into the biggest meltdown I had ever witnessed. It was a terrifying moment. She threw herself against the wall, hitting herself, and suddenly the bright, beautiful, happy little girl I knew seemed to disappear before my eyes. I didn't recognise the tear-soaked, distraught child in front of me. I broke down and just cried and cried until she finally stopped. In that heart-wrenching moment, I realised that I had to approach things differently. The typical "this is what we did with our kids" techniques weren't working for Ruby and us. It was a turning point in our journey, a moment when I realised that my daughter's unique needs demanded a unique approach.

As a first-time mother, the journey is never easy. We carry our own experiences and the wisdom from our childhood with us. We soak in advice from elders who've walked this path before, listen to well-meaning suggestions from friends and family, and then there's the wealth of expert advice available. Let's not forget the Pandora's box of information that is Google and the vast expanse of the internet. In the age of information overload, there are countless layers of advice and learning that inundate us. Sometimes, we absorb so much guidance that we forget to consider what truly resonates with us as a family, not to mention the fear of making any mistakes when it comes to raising a child. The world has structured itself into a system where neurotypical development is the norm; a system of learning, sharing, and repeating. But as our world rapidly evolves, it becomes increasingly clear that it's high time for a shift.

Around the age of 3, I began to wonder if I was seeing signs of OCD in Ruby. This was around the same time I found myself pregnant with my son, a bittersweet moment that came after another devastating miscarriage. My protective instincts were at an all-time high around both Ruby and my unborn son, and I couldn't help but notice behaviours in Ruby that felt different. I spoke to close family and friends about my concerns, hoping to find some reassurance, but I was met with dismissals. "She's so bright, you're just overthinking things and being too protective," became a familiar refrain. It was disheartening to have my worries brushed aside, and it left me feeling isolated in my concerns.

Seeking more guidance, I turned to a Health Visitor, hoping for some clarity. I expressed my thoughts about Ruby's potential regression from the age of 2 into 3, along with the emerging signs of OCD. To my disappointment, even the Health Visitor reassured me that Ruby was hitting all her developmental milestones. The piece of paper she held in her hand told us that Ruby's development was on track, and my concerns were dismissed as nothing more than overthinking.

I remember a holiday when I took my daughter to a kids' play centre. In one corner, there was a large Lego building section, and I watched my 3-year-old daughter and a little boy playing side by side, both busy constructing towers. As I observed, I couldn't help but notice a stark contrast. While both kids were happily building their towers, the little boy's creation was impressive, tall and grand. But what caught everyone's attention was my daughter's tower. Hers was just as tall, but it was meticulously colour-coordinated and perfectly symmetrical on both sides. People began to gather around, marvelling at her creation in amazement. In that moment, I realised something profound about my precious and special little girl, I knew she was talented in ways I was only just beginning to see and understand. It was a glimpse into her unique abilities, a preview of the remarkable journey that lay ahead, and a reminder that our children, especially those with special needs, have their own extraordinary gifts waiting to be discovered.

After my son's birth, my daughter's behaviour underwent a sudden transformation. The school noticed her new and "very disruptive behaviours," and it was during this time that a supply teacher who had only been with Ruby for two months suggested a referral for an Autism assessment. The teacher asked, "Do you give us permission to refer her?" I paused for what felt like an eternity, torn between saying yes and thinking, "Is this really happening?" The teacher's prompt came again, and this time, I said yes.

I hung up the phone and prepared to tell my husband. He reacted calmly, saying, "If you feel this is needed, then okay." I knew, in that moment, that his love for Ruby would cloud the truth that was looming on the horizon.

When my son turned six months, my heart already sensed something different. He was a wonderfully happy little guy, but I could see what the future was bringing already. I kept quiet at the time, and looking back, I wonder why. Was it guilt or shame, maybe a bit of both? Guilt for thinking he might be neurodivergent, guilt for creating a life that might need additional support. The thought of explaining this to my family, especially those who didn't yet know about Ruby's assessment, I felt completely overwhelmed. I stayed silent, using the excuse that he was too young, and the truth would only become clear as he got older.

At that moment, I believed our family was complete with two beautiful little heroes. But the universe had other plans. A surprise pregnancy whilst using contraception landed on our doorstep. I held the positive test and cried in shock, while my husband cried with joy. After four miscarriages, years of struggles, tears, and fertility treatments, I knew this was a gift to treasure. This baby would be the true completion of our family of heroes.

In November 2019, Ruby was finally diagnosed with Autism. I had already accepted what the diagnosis would be, but my husband, right up to the moment we walked into the room for the results, clung to the hope that it might be a mistake. When we left that room, he held me close, and his tears fell silently on my shoulder. The only words he could muster were, "my little girl, I really can't believe it," but those tears confirmed his acceptance of the truth.

As the denial faded, we embraced support systems, delved into reading, attended meetings, and worked tirelessly to get Ruby the support we felt she needed. Meanwhile, Phoenix was only 11 months old, and by this point, I had a growing conviction that he, too, would be diagnosed with Autism. I was also four months pregnant, carrying the secret of my son Phoenix, while trying to support Ruby as she settled into her reception class. Her behaviours evolved, and her Pathological Demand Avoidance (PDA) profile reached a new level that we struggled to comprehend.

During this tumultuous time, my father suffered his first heart attack, and we mourned the loss of my dear grandmother, who had believed that my soon-to-be-born daughter, Sienna Rose, was an angel and asked for her to be named Rose. Her sudden departure from our world shattered me to the core.

I remember sitting in nans favourite chair staring up at her Christmas tree that was at least 25 years old, cradling my belly, unable to shed tears. I felt an internal pain, but no tears would fall. The months that followed were a silent struggle as we tried to survive until my little miracle was due in March.

Little did we know that when we went to the hospital to welcome our new addition in March 2020, we would be stepping into day one of the first COVID lockdown, and our world would be thrown into chaos once again.

By the time Sienna Rose was born, I had already contacted the Health Visitor, seeking a referral for Phoenix. At 12 months, he regressed dramatically.

His words and eye contact seemed to vanish, and he began heavy rocking and constant stimming. Suddenly, he became extremely selective with food, noise, and busy spaces. I knew his diagnosis was imminent.

My husband had accepted Ruby's diagnosis and supported us through reading and learning, and we were gearing up for the next phase with Phoenix. However, this time, the support system didn't seem as straightforward. We faced more questions and objections, with some suggesting that he was just a boy and might be developing at his own pace. People said that I was comparing him to Ruby, who was exceptionally bright, which wasn't fair. They claimed the regression, stimming, and the lack of words or speech were normal, especially for boys.

I couldn't accept these explanations and continued to push for answers. Finally, when Phoenix was 18 months old, the Health Visitor agreed to see him for a second video call assessment. It wasn't until he was 22 months that the Health Visitor acknowledged that I might have been right all along, as Phoenix had made no progress since his 12-month developmental check-up.

At almost 3 years old, Phoenix was diagnosed with Autism and global delay. He was non-verbal and the happiest little guy, his smile capable of lighting up any room. At that point, I believed that with the diagnosis in hand, we could focus on providing our children with all the love and support they needed to grow into confident and happy adults; but I soon realised that our journey as parents of children with special needs would be fraught with challenges. The lack of support offered by our SEND UK system, the constant struggle for funding, the battle for the right school provision, and numerous other obstacles became part of our daily lives. However, I wanted to share my journey as a mother, a mother of children with special educational needs, in this chapter. The fight to advocate for my children is ongoing, and I'm fully aware that we have a long journey ahead. Nevertheless, I'm committed to being their voice until they find their own.

Caring for a child with additional needs has led to a profound transformation in me, in ways I could never have imagined. Motherhood alone shapes and moulds us, causing us to adapt and accept new roles. But becoming a SEND mum takes that transformation a step further, shedding some layers of our identity and replacing them with new ones. Every aspect of life undergoes change. Your parenting style, how you cook, clean, organise, speak, and even share your love with your child is altered. The way you approach daily routines, prepare for outings, host guests, or celebrate special events all takes on a new meaning as a SEND mother.

The traditions and ideas you held dear from your own upbringing shift in an instant when you recognise that the world is structured around neurotypical patterns and traditions that don't quite fit your neurodivergent family. Take Christmas, for example. We exchange fewer gifts or spread them throughout the season to avoid overwhelming our children. The Christmas dinner table may include bagels, pasta, toast, or even scrambled eggs on occasion, to accommodate their preferences. Christmas movies and TV shows are limited as we are often watching their favourite programmes and films on repeat. Our children, now 9, 4, and 3, haven't experienced family trips to see Santa or visited Christmas markets or places yet. Perhaps this year will be the one, or maybe not. What matters is that, when our family is ready, we'll embrace all the experiences they wish for. For now, we're letting go of traditional ideals and creating our own unique family traditions.

Being a SEND mother has been a journey of patience, compassion, understanding, and the continuous process of unlearning and relearning. It's a new experience entirely. Navigating the world of stimming, sensory processing, Pathological Demand Avoidance, OCD, anxiety, panic attacks, food avoidance, sleep routines (or the lack thereof), pre-verbal communication, learning Makaton, endless paperwork, meetings, and the relentless advocacy for your child, especially for things they should already be receiving, such as an education in the right school setting, is a monumental task.

Each of these elements adds a unique layer to my identity as a woman and a mother.

Currently, I'm awaiting the diagnosis for my tiniest hero, Sienna Rose. She's on a long waiting list, and this wait is just a part of the broken system we contend with every day.

Through it all, my three little heroes have been the most extraordinary teachers, and one of the most crucial lessons they've imparted is finding myself in this journey. It's all too easy to lose oneself as a mother, and even easier as a SEND mom, as our children require so much from us, and we want to give them everything. But in the midst of this, I've learned not to lose myself completely. We are here to experience life as individuals as well as mothers. Our identity is ours to shape, and we can still be the mother and the woman we choose to be, for ourselves and for our children. We have the ability to show them what it's like to live a life authentically as us, as you. We get to show them that you can be who you want to be and create what you desire in this life. We can choose to create our own path and show our heroes that they can to. There are no limits set for us or them.

Together, we always find a way; our way.

El Jedras

About the Author

El Jedras is a visionary leader, CEO of Evolveology® and Feminology UK Retreats. As an Intuitive Psychic and mindset coach, El guides transformative journeys for personal and business growth. Deeply committed to advocating for equal rights in special education, El actively engages with the SEND community, working on projects that aim to create a more inclusive and supportive environment.

El is a two-time best-selling author and a proud SEN mum of three little heroes. Her passion lies in empowering others to use their voice as a catalyst for change, shaping not only their own future but also influencing the path for others. All of this is done with a focus on preserving our authentic identity.

The Day The Sunshine Caught The Rain

The sun was shining just a moment ago,
But now here come the showers.
The washing is dripping, still on the line,
She thinks "well it's good for the flowers".

Most will rush to gather the shirts,
To put on the airer to dry.
But she looks up to see all the colours,
That are starting to fill the sky.

Red, orange, green and blue,
She wonders what lies at the end.
Then reminds herself to be patient,
Much like her journey with SEND.

In a blink of an eye the rainbow is gone,
Only soggy socks remain.
But the memory will last forever,
The day the sunshine caught the rain.

Chelle Cox

Glossary

Unlock the language of our stories with this handy glossary, providing explanations for the abbreviations used throughout our heartfelt journey into SEND motherhood.

ASD – Autism Spectrum Disorder: A neurodevelopmental disorder characterised by persistent patterns of social communication and interaction challenges and restricted, repetitive behaviours.

ADHD – Attention Deficit Hyperactivity Disorder: A neurodevelopmental disorder characterised by persistent patterns of inattention, impulsivity, and hyperactivity that can interfere with daily functioning or development.

CAMHS – Child and Adolescent Mental Health Services: This is an NHS service that provides mental health support, assessments, and treatments for children and adolescents.

CYPMHS – Children and Young People's Mental Health Services: Similar to CAMHS, this service provides mental health support, assessments, and treatments for children and adolescents.

CBT – Cognitive Behavioural Therapy: A widely used therapeutic approach that focuses on identifying and changing negative thought patterns and behaviours.

Dyscalculia: A learning disability that impairs a person's ability to comprehend and work with numbers, affecting mathematical understanding and skills.

EBSA – Emotional Based School Avoidance: A term used to describe those who have difficulty attending school due to emotional distress, anxiety, or other emotional challenges.

EHCP – Educational Health and Care Plan: A legal document that sets out the education, healthcare, and social needs of a child or young person who requires additional support in school beyond what the school can provide.

GDD - Global Developmental Delay: A term used when a child doesn't reach developmental milestones within the expected range across various areas such as motor skills, speech, cognitive abilities, and social skills.

Makaton – A communication language program that uses signs and symbols to support individuals with communication difficulties, aiding both verbal and non-verbal communication.

Meltdown – An intense response to stress or sensory overload, often associated with conditions like autism. It involves a loss of emotional regulation and may include difficulty communicating and self-soothing behaviours.

OCD – Obsessive-Compulsive Disorder: A mental health condition where a person has obsessive thoughts and compulsive behaviours.

PDA – Pathological Demand Avoidance: Widely understood to be a profile on the Autism Spectrum, involving the avoidance of everyday demands and requests. Those with PDA may use various strategies to resist and control situations, often stemming from anxiety and a need for control.

PECS – Picture Exchange Communication System: A visual communication method for individuals with challenges in verbal communication, especially those with autism.

Rainbow Baby: A term used to describe a baby born after a pregnancy or infant loss, such as a miscarriage, stillbirth, or neonatal death. The rainbow symbolizes hope and healing, representing the beauty that follows the storm of loss.

SEND – Special, Educational Needs and Disabilities: This term encompasses a range of learning difficulties and disabilities that require support in an educational setting.

SPD – Sensory Processing Disorder: A condition where the brain has difficulty receiving and responding to information received through the senses.

Stim/Stimming – Refers to self-stimulatory behaviours, often involving repetitive movements or sounds.

Tic: A sudden, repetitive, nonrhythmic motor movement or vocalisation. Tics are often associated with conditions like Tourette's syndrome but can also occur in other disorders.

As we conclude 'The Journey into SEND Motherhood: Finding the End of the Rainbow,' our heart overflows with gratitude. Thank you for embracing these stories, for allowing the essence of SEND motherhood into your lives with open minds and tender hearts.

To the remarkable mothers who shared their journeys, your courage and authenticity have woven a tapestry of strength and resilience. May your narratives be a beacon of inspiration and solace to those threading similar paths.

To every reader, know that you are not alone. In the moments of challenge, find comfort in our shared experiences, and in the victories, celebrate the extraordinary strength within you.

With profound gratitude,
S.E.N.D Reform England

For continued support and resources, please visit www.sendreformengland.com

Printed in Great Britain
by Amazon

34468612R00099